MW00616915

FIND MORE
STRENGTH

FIND MORE STRENGTH

*5 Pillars to Unlock Unlimited
Power & Happiness*

PAMELA PALLADINO GOLD

FIND MORE STRENGTH
5 Pillars to Unlock Unlimited Power & Happiness
Pamela Palladino Gold

Copyright © 2016
No part of this book may be reproduced or
transmitted in any form by any means, electronic,
mechanical, photocopying, recording, or otherwise,
without the prior written
permission of the author.

The information provided in this book is designed
to provide helpful information about the subjects
discussed. The author and publisher disclaim any
and all liability associated with the recommendations
and guidelines set forth in this book. There are no
guarantees implied or expressed from the information
or principles contained in this book. Individual results
will vary.

Printed in the United States of America
ISBN-13: 978-0692843307 (Gold Evolution)
ISBN-10: 0692843302

TABLE OF CONTENTS

Dedicated to my Gram. You are always with me.

ACKNOWLEDGEMENTS

There are so many people without whom this book would not have been possible. In no particular order, and in deepest gratitude, here they are:

My husband, Roger, who has been my greatest spiritual teacher. He has a lion heart and is the most dedicated person I know. My daughter, Talia, who from the time she was one and a half would engage with me on all of this, and GOT IT. I never could've imagined a young person so wise and strong and her love and companionship humbles me. My son, Jesse, who like me is an experiential learner and frequently gets frustrated with me, yelling, "I don't believe what you believe, mom!" to which I lovingly reply "I get it buddy, you gotta figure it all out for yourself." He is fierce with a huge heart and will grow to be a strong, loving man. My mom, who has more grit than anyone I could imagine and who taught me to work hard, take full responsibility for myself and "the power of positive thinking" among many, many other things. My dad, who was always the philosopher and problem solver, taught me never to stop asking questions and looking for deeper answers, connections and patterns. He has been my biggest champion.

Don Baba for teaching me magic. Josh for bravely owning his story and allowing me to share some of it. Erin for being the best friend and angel I could've imagined. Pattie for all your love and strength. Sylwia for teaching me to find my strength. Jane and Jeff for your support, creativity and generosity. Irina for your time, talent and friendship. Anika for the years of your love and support. Amal for your trust, feedback, support and friendship. Leona for being the first person to say, I'll read it and for your comments. Deste for your friendship and graphic design skilz. Whit for somehow seeing the diamond in the rough and being so brilliant inspiring and supportive all these years. Peter for organizing amazing people who inspire and empowered me. Mel for being an absolute rockstar. Laura for your brilliance. I couldn't have gotten through these last few months without all of you.

Carolyn Myss, Eckert Tolle, Byron Katie, Mooji, Yogananda, Hariharinanda, Ali Berlin, Alan Finger, Peter Ferko, Ali Cramer, Dr. Martin Seligman, Dr. Dan Siegel, Dr. David Hawkins, Brene Brown, Angela Duckworth, K. Anders Ericsson, Dr. Rick Hanson, Alan Watts, Richard Bach, Vishen Lakhiani, Brian Johnson, Dan Harris, Sharon Salzberg, Tara Brach, Mike Dooley, to name just a few of the brilliant teachers I have been lucky enough to learn from.

I am deeply humbled and grateful for all that has allowed me to be who I am.

"A Strong Spirit Can Break All Rules."

– Prince

PROLOGUE

I grew up on my grandfather's apple farm, in small town upstate New York. There were two different spots on the farm that I always loved to go when I needed to get away—one up on the hill off to the south, one of the highest parts of the area for miles, where I could sit and watch the sunset over Mohonk without a single house or road in sight. The other, on the west part of the farm behind my house, had a slight dip in the landscape that also provided seclusion from any other signs of human life. I could sit among the apple trees and pretend that I was the only person in the world, while feeling connected to something much, much bigger. I naturally gravitated to those spots when I needed to find more strength. And I always found it there.

INTRODUCTION

Life isn't easy, and it's never, ever going to be painless. The challenges, whether we appreciate them or not, however poorly timed or seemingly cruel, are always what give us the opportunity to grow. Unfortunately, it seems to me that the fundamental problem with being human is that we are wired for survival . . . and so many of the "survival instincts" that we are born with and that develop through conditioning, are actually working against us when it comes to reaching our highest potential and living a happy life.

At the root of it, our brain's desire to keep us safe and feel *good enough* turns into the impulse to stay *comfortable*—I see it in my 8 year old when he doesn't want to go to Tae Kwon Do because it's out of his comfort zone. I see it in myself when I drag my feet jumping back into a tough exercise routine after some time away. We may know intellectually that getting out of our comfort zone is how we grow, but the awareness and skill that we need to do it effectively is *hard*. Similarly, our desire to *belong*, which translates into the struggle of feeling *good enough*, keeps us subconsciously feeling overwhelmed by the inherent messiness of the challenges in our lives. The stress, anxiety and self criticism keep us stuck in "survival mode" when really, our actual survival isn't really threatened at all.

I wanted to know the difference between the people who are thriving and fulfilled in their lives and those who are not. Between those who feel like life is merely about survival so much of the time and those who are out there living full lives.

I believe that people who are thriving feel safe, feel connected, and feel *good enough*. So what is going on with those people that they are in that state, instead of feeling unsafe, disconnected and/or not worthy of love? What are their lives like? Is it possible that they don't have challenges like the rest of us? Or are they perhaps able to tap into something when the challenges come that enables them to continually rise up, instead of getting beaten down?

This book is for anyone who wants the answers to those questions. Anyone who feels like they are often surviving, instead of thriving. Anyone who wants to feel happier, more empowered and more fulfilled in their lives. Anyone who wants to achieve real, lasting greatness in all areas of their life.

* * *

It's always seemed pretty obvious to me that I wanted to get stronger, instead of weaker.

From the time I was little, I was fiercely confident and curious. I basically wanted to figure everything out to make sure that I could always get what I wanted. My mom loves telling the story about how when I was barely walking, I taught my older brother to move a chair over to get up on the counter and get the cookies. Needless to say, I consistently got myself into a lot of trouble over the years.

I didn't understand when I was younger the different types of strength, and that in some ways what may've seemed strong was actually weak . . . Bullying someone, for example—when I was little, I didn't understand that not caring about someone else's feelings and just forcing them to do what I wanted wasn't actually strong—it only seems that way on the surface of course. If you can look deeper, you can see the damage that it causes and the weakness that it comes from. I learned that lesson in 5th grade, when my core group of friends all were angry with me and excluded me from their circle, and a group of other girls who I hadn't ever been particularly nice to were so kind to me and included me in their activities—the lesson of the power of kindness deeply implanted itself into my being from that point on.

As I got older, I kept "leveling up" on my understanding of strength, and the meaning of life, and I've come to realize that inner strength is where our power really comes from. Power to be used for good, in harmony with all that is going on around us, to make our world a brighter place.

When I use the term "leveling up" I am referring to the shifts that come with both epiphanies and skill level advancement, and there are five overarching levels that I will describe later on in the book: Victim, Hero, Power of Thoughts, Service and Oneness. I started out in both the Victim and Hero levels, bouncing around depending on the situation, and the epiphanies and skills that now allow me to mainly reside in the higher levels are very much the subject of this book.

I truly owe all of my growth to my teachers. I had formal teachers, ranging from the work of Alan Watts, Michael Singer, Caroline Myss, Mooji, Hariharananda, Yogananda, Jack Kornfield (to name just a few) and classes with Don Baba, Alan Finger, Ali Cramer, Jason Vinci, Peter Ferko, Mona Anand, Molly Carmel (again, just a few examples), who taught me concepts and skills and shined the light on where I needed to go to find the truths for myself. But many of my "best" teachers came in the form of the people in my day to day life. The deeper the relationship, the more opportunity we have to learn from it. Our parents, our partners, our children, our closest friends. It is these relationships that are inherently both the most formative and the most triggering, and provide long term, deeper challenges. If we bravely own our issues and commit to improving our skills, our personal evolution will be the path to keep the relationship healthy or to forgive and accept as we move on, whichever is meant to be. Both paths will lead us to a deeper personal peace and greater Spiritual Strength, if we can bravely do the required work.

At the end of the day, my expertise comes from direct experience. That experience is the cement that allows my intellectual and theoretical learning to take hold. If you wanted to ask someone to give you recommendations on visiting Paris, would you ask someone who has read a lot of books on Paris or would you ask someone who lived there for 20 years? Of course, direct experience always beats theoretical learning.

Philosophy, spiritual texts, all of the hard sciences, business, political science, parenting, psychology, and wellness were all areas of study that I loved and pursued with reckless abandon. With the exception of the fugue of being a new parent (during which I did read a lot of parenting books, but that was about it), I have always been a voracious reader. It started with incredibly inappropriate fiction at too young of an age, but quickly moved to topics like quantum physics, Eastern religion, history, international politics, psychology and philosophy, before I even really understood what all of those things were. I was always raised in a home that subscribed to the Skeptical Inquirer, a bi-weekly magazine the debunked anything that couldn't be proven. So, reading that as a kid grounded me in the mentality that something needed to be proven to be believed.

My studies kept bringing me deeper in questioning what I could know to be true, and at the same time, learning more and more practices that gave me the strength and skill to live my best life—I experienced strong, loving relationships and then faced extreme challenges to their health. I had the opportunity to figure out how and when to heal them. And most importantly, that includes my relationship with myself. It is this personal experience that has connected the dots on all of the formal teaching I've had over the years, and has brought me to the knowledge in this book and the synthesis of the 5 Pillars.

Sharing this knowledge with anyone who it resonates with, either now, in two years, five years, lifetimes from now, is my mission—it is life changing to figure out how to reach inner peace and the power that comes with it. Inner peace is the ultimate strength.

Especially when the going gets tough, we need strength to handle whatever life throws at us. Strength to stay calm, clear and proactive to make our situation better, instead of worse. So the million dollar question is how do we get stronger? How do we find more strength in those particularly hard moments, when we really need it? How do we handle what is legitimately hard, painful and overwhelming, with grace, ease and ninja-like effectiveness? Rising up instead of getting weighed down?

Physical Strength and Mental Strength

In all ways, we want to Find More Strength.
We are really clear on how we get stronger physically. We run, bike, workout with a trainer, exercise our muscles,

our balance, our agility—we purposely practice, set goals and keep increasing them.

Experience tells us that practice makes progress: we get stronger, faster, more nimble. We can lift heavier weights, jump higher, go for longer . . . stretch and balance in ways that we couldn't before . . . in any given moment, our best is better than it was the day before. We get stronger.

Same thing for mental exercise: we know that we can read, study, watch documentaries, practice various types of problem solving . . . and with purposeful practice, our mental strength will increase. There is so much advanced research on the most effective ways to study, how we learn. If we look at a chess player, for example, we can see how training and strengthening occurs. The more hours they spend studying, the more complex their understanding of all of the possibilities, more and more moves ahead.

Again, experience tells us that practice makes progress: we can solve tougher mental challenges quicker and with greater accuracy . . . we can see more steps ahead, untangle complexities in ways that we couldn't before. Have more complex, accurate mental representations of what we are trying to solve. At any given moment, our best is better than it was the day before. We get stronger.

It is obvious how powerful it is to be physically and mentally stronger, and while it takes hard work, we recognize how important it is to prioritize that work and how it is worth the effort to make our lives as great as possible.

Spiritual Strength

One of my favorite professors at Yale, Allan Stam, started his first lecture by making a triangle with his fingers and saying SKILLS, KNOWLEDGE, ATTITUDE. His point was, to achieve greatness, we needed to focus on all three.

Skills: what we are capable of doing.
Knowledge: what we know to be true.
Attitude: how we look at our situation.

In my experience, all three are critical to achieve real, lasting greatness in anything that we do.

Skills are developed by practice, with the formula Talent × Effort = Skills. Hard work beats talent when talent doesn't work hard! Take any discipline from sports to music to academics and this is true. Both Angela Duckworth in her book *Grit* and Anders Ericsson in his book *Peak: Secrets from the New Science of Expertise* give extensive research from countless disciplines backing this up. Ballet, violin, short term memory, chess—you name it, effort is the controllable key in developing our skills.

Knowledge is developed by learning facts—the deeper your knowledge of any subject, the more capable you will be of working within that space to achieve any desired results. Again, take any discipline or activity and it is clear that knowledge is power. If someone were to ask you to go get milk, and you were in your hometown and you had knowledge of the area, of the stores, of the currency, it would be easy to do it. If you were in the middle of a foreign country where you didn't know the word for milk, didn't know where there were stores, didn't know anything about the currency, it would be really hard to go buy milk. Knowledge is power.

Attitude is your mindset or how you are looking at your situation. A positive attitude is looking at things as possible, feeling capable of achieving positive results, believing in the possibilities. A negative attitude on the other hand is looking for and believing in negative outcomes. Our attitude dictates the thoughts we are having and feeding, either positive thoughts or negative thoughts, and research consistently shows the power of a positive attitude on both outcomes and health benefits.[1] In other words, our thoughts impact our reality. Change your thoughts, change your reality.

When we look at our attitude and what determines our attitude, or what is the underlying force of our attitude, I see one thing:

Our Spirit.

When I say Spirit, I mean, this inner energetic sense of how are we feeling . . . At first it feels inseparable from our emotional being, but it actually is more subtle than that.

---

[1] LYUBOMIRSKY, KING, AND DIENER, The Benefits of Frequent Positive Affect: Does Happiness Lead to Success? Psychological Bulletin, American Psychological Association 2005, Vol. 131, No. 6, 803–855.

When someone asks you, "How are your spirits?" You know what they mean, right? They are asking how you are feeling, and we think about our emotions. If we are happy, feeling positive, energized, lighthearted and loving, we say our spirits are "great", or "high". If we are feeling lousy, sad, or depressed, we would say that we are feeling low or blue, or our spirits aren't so good. In any given moment, our spirit is at a certain level.

There are three elements that are present when we feel "happy": appreciation, positivity and openness. When we aren't feeling happy, if we check in with gratitude, positivity (which requires faith and/or courage), and openness, I am certain at least one will be missing. And obviously, when we are unhappy, our spirits aren't "great", and the "lowness" that we feel actually is a weakened state.

The connection between Spirit and Attitude is undeniable. If our Spirits are positive, our mindset or attitude will be positive . . . but as our Spirits drop, our mindset or attitude turns negative as well. So the question is, how positive is our Spirit? And, how **Strong is our Spirit**? How much can we take before we go from having a positive attitude to a negative attitude? How much pain, heartbreak, negativity and exhaustion can we endure before we say, "I can't do this." ? How many challenges, disappointments, injustices, tragedies (aka triggers) can we take before we say, "I can't handle this."? How able are we to keep our spirits up, going from setback to setback without losing hope or enthusiasm?[2]

This is Spiritual Strength

A Strong Spirit is even more important than a strong body or a strong mind, and here's why: It is the getting back up when you get knocked down, and HOW FAST you get back up, no matter how hard or how many times you get knocked down. It is how deep you dig, how committed you are to not giving up, to finding the answer or the way. It is how brave, resilient and gritty you are. It is how flexible, adaptable, creative and inspired you are. It is how appreciative you are. It is how calm and clear and precise you are. All of this is Strength of Spirit.

Look at Bethany Hamilton, the surfing prodigy who at 13 lost her arm in a shark attack. She was back on her surf board a month later and continued towards her dream of becoming a pro surfer. And yes, she achieved it.

Not as extreme but equally significant given the career that followed, Michael Jordan was cut from the basketball team his sophomore year of high school. Instead of giving up, he worked harder and went on to become a 5 time MVP and Hall of Famer who dominated basketball for a decade.

---

[2]Winston Churchill: Success is the ability to move from failure to failure without losing enthusiasm.

J.K. Rowling was a single mother relying on state subsidies when she was writing *Harry Potter*, and the manuscript was rejected 12 times before one of the publishers decided to give it a chance. Look at what sticking with it brought—a franchise now worth an estimated $15B and, more importantly as far as I am concerned, millions of inspired people.

So what allows people to persevere through painful, scary and overwhelming times with as much grace as possible? When I say *Spiritual Strength*, I mean being in that position of inner power. It is how positive we are feeling and how much we can take and still feel positive. Are we overcoming our fear? Are we feeling worthy of love? Are we feeling confident, creative, open? Able to continue moving forward? True happiness, happiness "for no reason" comes from this state of inner strength. And, at any given moment, we can tap into "more strength", if we know how.

That *inner strength* is what enables us to BE the highest force of love and creation and achievement that we can be. If we don't find that strength and our spirits drop, we can't be our best selves. Everyone around us feels it, our work shows it. We aren't bold, we aren't kind and generous, we aren't creative, we aren't present . . . We can't be visionaries and break the rules, that's for sure. We will play it safe. We will downplay our greatness, because we don't FEEL our greatness.

**We can't BE great without having Strength of Spirit.
So how do we find it when we lose it?**

Fortunately, just like physical strength and mental strength, practice makes progress. By breaking down the components of Spiritual Strength, we can train our Spirit in the same way we train our body and our mind. Practicing when it isn't "Game On", meaning the going hasn't gotten too tough, is the key to success. A tennis player would never go into a big match with out practicing and expect to do great, and the same goes for spiritual strength. Practice regularly, day in and day out, and you will find more strength when the going gets tough.

Spiritual Practice Game Plan:

1. Gratitude
2. Compassion
3. Courage
4. Surrender
5. Openness/Curiosity

I call these the 5 Pillars and the following chapters will review each in depth ... and this is the name of the spiritual game. Gratitude, Compassion, Courage, Surrender and Openness/Curiosity all work together like parts of the same wheel and we can (and need to!) work on all of them at the same time. Each supports the other and as you make strides in each area you will feel yourself "leveling up".

Gratitude is the first, and perhaps there is a first only because in our linear world we need to go in order ... but first is Gratitude because I feel like it is the root system of our strength.

Ever since I was a kid I've been a bit obsessed with trees . . . maybe it has to do with growing up on the apple farm, running around and climbing trees . . . or maybe it is because there is a powerful analogy found in a tree that always seemed to resonate with how I was figuring out my life.

If you wanted to have a strong, healthy tree, you needed big, strong roots, which of course you can't see. But if a tree grows too big without strong roots, it is toast. The bigger the tree, the bigger the roots need to be, or it will fall right over. And of course the roots provide sustenance for the tree, besides just the grounding force.

Then there is the trunk, also obviously critical to the strength and health of the tree, providing the infrastructure of everything that it is out in the world.

And then, the branches and leaves, growing, reaching out, every expanding, representing all that the tree *does*. Flower, bear fruit, grow leaves, make food for the tree . . .

I use the tree analogy so often in trying to understand something that is nonlinear, because all parts of the tree are simultaneously flourishing, and one could not exist without the others.

It is the same way for the 5 pillars that we will be reviewing—each needs to develop in harmony with the others in order for the growth to be balanced and the tree (you) to flourish.

So, Gratitude comes first, because it is like the roots, grounding us and providing sustenance.

Next comes Compassion, which I describe as the life force itself, providing the flow of energy connecting each part of the tree and what IS the flow of life in the tree.

Courage is next, which provides the framework or infrastructure to enable life and growth—like the trunk if you are following me here on my tree.

Then we have Surrender which is critical to have any new growth—we can think of it as the old falling away to make way for the new. If a tree were to hold on as it naturally cycled through the seasons, never letting its seeds fall, never being pruned, it wouldn't be able to have new growth. In the same way, as much as our mind really, really doesn't want to Surrender, it is precisely that which we need to do in order to be able to grow and be healthy, to really flourish.

And last, but definitely not least, we have Openness and Curiosity, which is the new growth, new buds, new branches, growing where there was only unknown before.

As we go through each pillar in detail, we will have a deeper understanding of what they really mean, the ways that we typically get stuck, and most importantly, the ways that we can practice them to make progress. These are skills that with effort we can get better at mastering. In the end, if you get ninja-like with these 5 pillars, you will find more strength than you can imagine. You can literally unlock unlimited power and happiness.

Part 1

The Five Pillars

Chapter 1

GRATITUDE

I don't have to chase extraordinary moments to find happiness - it's right in front of me if I'm paying attention and practicing gratitude.

— Brené Brown

There is, arguably, nothing more foundational to Spiritual Strength than Gratitude. Just like a tree cannot be strong without its roots, we cannot be strong without Gratitude . . . and Gratitude is the base of where our Spiritual Strength "begins".

I describe Gratitude as feeling lucky. Feeling blessed. Feeling or appreciating an incoming flow of opportunity or "goodness". That feeling is so deep and so powerful when we really connect to it, it literally roots us to power and strength.

It's pretty obvious how important Gratitude is, but that doesn't mean it is easy.

The Challenge of Gratitude

It's really, really hard for our mind to look into the face of pain or challenges and feel lucky. Our lower, reptilian brain sees the world in basic terms. Pain = Bad, Pleasure = Good. Struggle = Bad, Success = Good. Hard = Bad, Easy = Good. The more time we spend in our higher brain, the more we can see that things aren't that simple. Research has shown time and time again that we need to have struggle for growth . . . That failures are stepping stones to greatness. So the more we can stay in our higher brain, the more we can be grateful in the face of pain or challenges.

The tricky thing is, pain automatically puts us into our Sympathetic Nervous System or what we call Fight or Flight mode. We go into our lower brain for survival to react quickly. Fight or Flight, however, is not growth and appreciation mode . . . So if we want to be able to stare pain in the face and skillfully learn as much as we can from it instead of fighting or running from it, we are going to need to work to rewire our brains. That is how we can remember to focus on growth and how we can remember to feel grateful regardless of the pain.

Tragedy and Gratitude

People have often asked, how can you possibly propose to feel grateful in the face of tragedy? Like, for example, Sandy Hook? How can you say to the parents who lost their sweet 6 year old children to be GRATEFUL?

I know how it sounds. My daughter was in 1st Grade at the same time that the Sandy Hook shooting happened. Friday, December 14, 2012 was the first time my husband

I left our kids to travel by plane for a weekend away. We arrived at the airport, got to our gate, and saw on TV the reports of what was happening . . . and the news that twenty 6 and 7 year olds were murdered along with six adult staff members. I sat on the floor by the gate and sobbed. I called my parents who were heading to our kids' school to pick them up and just sobbed. I am not capable of truly imagining the pain of losing a child, but I am certain that there is no greater pain a human can endure.

I am not saying it is easy or even HUMAN, but this is where Spiritual Strength is found. Pain is the touchstone of all growth, and the deeper the pain, the more of an opportunity we have to grow. It is all about our ability to process the pain, and for particularly tragic events, it may take a long time . . . staying in a humble place of gratitude will help us move through the pain quicker and grow in the ways we are meant to grow. If not grateful for the pain or tragedy and accompanying growth, then focus on feeling grateful for the gift of the joy that preceded the pain, however tragically it was taken away. And acceptance for the truth of how things currently are . . . more on that when we get to Courage and Surrender.

I have imagined losing my children more times than I can count, and have sobbed putting my kids to sleep imagining delivering their eulogy and standing at their funeral as the casket is lowered into the ground. I know it sounds sadistic, but fear of death, not just our own but anyone that we love, is one of the things that holds us back from really living life. Even before I figured out everything that I am writing in this book, I instinctively knew this . . . and I made myself fully face it.

I also am blessed to have a dear friend and mentor in life, a teacher who first taught me in Middle School and continued to care for me through High School when my mom was ill and through college when the boy I fell in love with was ill . . . giving me her love and spiritual support when I truly lost my own . . . this brilliant woman who will always hold her own private place in my heart, tragically lost her 21 year old daughter in a car accident and at the time my daughter was a year and half old. I remember getting the news about her daughter's death as I held my pumpkin in my arms and there was this intense transference of appreciation of how much of a gift our children are. We are not entitled to ANYTHING to come out of our love and all-nighters. We are not entitled to see them grow up. We are not entitled to see them get married. We are not entitled to have grandchildren. We are not entitled to one single moment with them other than the present one. This resonated to the deepest level of my soul and I remember it every day. This is gratitude for each moment with them and surrendering that this will all end someday.

The Shark Story

I remember shortly after graduating college, I was working at Cosi in the days before Facebook (!!) when the only way stories were shared or went viral was via email. My friends and I would pass around the content that inspired us or made us laugh with the tediousness of typing in everyone's emails when we wanted to share. It's funny to remember now but I do remember clearly getting this really inspirational email with this story about Japanese fishermen who were trying to bring back the freshest, highest quality fish to the fish market.

The story went something like, at first the fishermen tried freezing the fish but the customers could tell the difference between fresh and frozen fish . . . so next they tried keeping the fish alive in a tank to be brought back to market . . . but being kept in a static, tight environment like that, the fish didn't move, and again the customers reported that the fish didn't taste fresh. So then the fishermen tried putting a small shark in the tank with the fish, which obviously meant that some of the fish would be eaten by the shark, but it kept all of the fish active . . . and when they got to the fish market, the customers reported that those fish tasted very fresh and delicious.

Now, obviously this is a somewhat morbid story because all of the fish eventually end up being food, one way or another . . . but the point is that challenges keep us really living . . . fully ALIVE. There is this beautiful sweet spot where we keep trying to avoid getting eaten by sharks AND we are able to avoid getting eaten by sharks. . . . and we live our best life. Or, put another way, we have enough challenges in our life to keep us growing, but not too much that they break us. But we don't want to be afraid of breaking, either.

Courage and Gratitude

It goes without saying that Courage is super important in improving our Gratitude practice. As we will cover in detail when we get to the Chapter on Courage and as already mentioned, we need to get ninja-like skillfully facing our fears. If we are unskillfully swept away in our Fight or Flight response, we'll lose connection with Gratitude. The more painful and frightening the situation, the harder it will be, so we need to commit to practicing day in and day out when it is *easy* so we have a more automatic, reflexive response when it is *hard*.

Practicing Gratitude

Imagining our worst fears will indeed help us be grateful for our blessings, as will paying attention to the inequalities that are all around us. We are privileged if we have a healthy body. We are privileged if we have food and water . . . and on and on . . . if we practice noticing our blessings and FEELING grateful as we go about our day, we will be rewiring our brain to have more pathways to Gratitude, when we need it.

The more we make ourselves FEEL grateful, as we go about our day to day routines, the more we are paving the way for our mind to feel grateful automatically, as

a reflex. The more we do it with intention, the easier it gets to have it happen automatically.

There are so many ways to practice gratitude, and I recommend starting with one daily practice and adding on or switching it up as needed. But, practice everyday. Just like you brush and floss your teeth every day. Hopefully.

You can use an app on your phone to ping with you reminders to think about what you are grateful for and WHY you are grateful for it. The feelings associated with gratitude are what is so important to practice—just thinking of what you are grateful for without thinking of WHY you are grateful doesn't give you the feeling of gratitude and it is the feeling that is so important to be practicing.

Example: I am grateful for my children. That is pretty freaking obvious and that thought comes to mind in a nanosecond. Easy peasy. Not much even really happens feeling wise. If I make myself answer WHY I am grateful for my family ... I start to think about the snuggles, the "I love yous", their eyes lighting up with joy, the parenting gold moments when they overcome an obstacle or are spontaneously kind to someone ... my heart fills and I feel this deep feeling of gratitude—whereas just thinking about being thankful for my family was just like, yeah, what else is new? No big deal. You gotta go for the feeling. That connection. It's a game changer.

You can write in a gratitude journal before bed, again not just what you are grateful for, but WHY. Three things that you are grateful for, three things that went right that day.

You can start each day with an exclamation of gratitude. Sounds ridiculous, but I promise it will make your days brighter.

You can get in the habit of always connecting with something you are grateful for when you get in the car.

You can get in the habit of looking for and spotting little things that spark joy and calling them out. Sunsets! Pretty clouds! Cute baby! Furry dog! Beautiful tree! Someone smiled! Again, sounds ridiculous, but it is a great way to go about your day. All of that positive energy is contagious in a really good way, and people will feel your positivity and be more likely to be generous with you, I promise . . . not that this is why you are doing it, but it is a real benefit! And as for the people who are cranky and find your positivity annoying, well we need to surrender that those aren't our people.

You can play the gratitude game with your family, getting everyone to take a turn sharing what they are grateful for and specifically WHY. If you have kids, ask them to describe details and feelings!

Start to catch yourself when things go wrong - stop and find something to be grateful for . . . because it could ALWAYS be worse. Make yourself replace a complaint or exclamation of frustration with a "well, at least . . ." statement. At first, you will rarely catch yourself, but you consistently keep interjecting earlier and earlier, "Well, at least..." and find something positive to add to keep things in perspective.

Example: My daughter was getting herself milk out of the fridge the other day and a huge amount spilled. Since my mind now automatically responds to a feeling of frustration with "well, at least..." that starts to come out as I consciously look for something positive to add to the statement. In this case at first I said, "Well, at least . . . it didn't get all over everything INSIDE the fridge." Then she showed me that it did. So then I said, "Well, at least . . . it didn't get all into the veggie drawer!" and then she showed me that it did. So I settled with "Well, at least we aren't in a rush to get somewhere!" And we cleaned it up together.

If you are into praying, just take time to pray simple deep gratitude. Don't ask for anything. Just say thank you for all of the blessings in your life, instead of asking for things to be better.

And it may go without saying, but, eliminate complaints from your repertoire. Catch the thoughts before they leave your mouth. No more. Zero complaint policy. If you need support, and need to vent to process pain, that is one thing. But complaints out of habit, get rid of them. They are the opposite, literally, of gratitude. They are torpedoing your Spiritual Strength.

Another way of looking at gratitude is training your attention to focus on the positive. There is always a positive, as long as you are breathing - even when the pain is overwhelming or seemingly unbearable. Gratitude is one of the skills that will give you the strength to move through it.

Another example: I cut the F- out of my finger last night. I was opening up and cutting an avocado without being particularly careful, and I wanted to get the pit out so stabbed it really hard with a super sharp knife. The knife slipped off the pit and sliced my finger. It was a significant cut, and it really hurt, but the immediate thought in my head was, "Wow, I got lucky! That could've been REALLY bad!" My mind didn't even focus for a nanosecond on the negative, it immediately found the bright side. Thank you Gratitude practice for rewiring my brain to a no-bitching zone. And from that place I calmly assessed the situation (no stitches needed! woot!) and dealt with it. Without freaking out my kids.

GRATITUDE BONUS:

X Marks the Spot for Ridiculous Magic to Happen

You know the treasure maps where X marks the spot to find treasure? Gratitude is X Marks the Spot for abundance and blessings. If you stay in a place of gratitude, that is exactly where you need to be in time, space and energy to have the craziest most unexpected blessings and synchronicities fall on your lap. It may sound weird, but let's think about what it is like to be around someone who is grateful. Imagine you are spending the day with a kid and you have already done a few nice things for them, not big or anything, just typical lunch, maybe a treat. If the kid is super, sincerely grateful for everything you have done, you will feel like you naturally want to do more for them. It won't even be a logical thing, it'll just be how you feel. On the other hand, if the kid was unappreciative and complaining, you naturally would feel like NOT doing anything more for them. Your mind will chime in, but I promise that this would simply be a FEELING at the root of it. That FEELING is spiritual law, and it isn't just limited to how we treat each other. There is more to it, that we can't see or explain, but I promise you that FEELING grateful opens up the flow of blessings into your life.

Practice makes progress, so practice Gratitude.

CHAPTER 2

COMPASSION

"We must combine the toughness of the serpent with the softness of the dove, a tough mind and a tender heart."

— Martin Luther King

Compassion, is caring about others' well being—***being caring***. This is a feeling or an energetic state, and doesn't necessarily mean *doing anything*. Understanding what Compassion really is, as opposed to what we may think it is, is really important. People often think of Compassion as kindness, and it can be—but it isn't that simple.

A friend asked me to clarify this today actually: if you run into a beggar on the street, asking for money, the Compassionate thing would be to give them money, right? Not necessarily. You can't think through Compassion, it is something that needs to be felt, and each moment, each situation, is different. And, being present in that moment is key.

Compassion comes from the heart, not the mind

We FEEL Compassion, that is how we know it is there. You can sometimes see it in action, but you can't ever really see the spirit behind which someone does something kind, so you can't ever REALLY see it with your eyes. (sometimes something that seems kind is actually done out of judgment—more on that in a few)

One of my favorite quotes from when I was a kid, The Little Prince: "It is only with the heart that one can see rightly, what is essential is invisible to the eye." I remember reading that and feeling to the core of my being that it was true. I didn't understand how, but I KNEW it was true.

When it comes to Compassion, we need to get out of our head and into our heart, where we can sense what is *Right* (defined as what feels true for us, truly Brave, Wise and Compassionate—this is different than "right" vs. "wrong"). Sometimes it is action, sometimes it is inaction, but it always feels like love. Openhearted Love.

So often people equate Compassion with weakness, that by caring someone will have something over you or you will be vulnerable to being taken advantage of or you will not be ready to respond to a threat. This couldn't be farther from the truth.

True Compassion universally brings strength because it means that your heart is open and there is a flow of positivity that you can USE for your OWN good. It actually doesn't have anything to do with doing something for anyone else—it always benefits and empowers you! The spiritual reality is that if anything truly benefits you, it also benefits others and vice versa. If you close your heart, which feels like not caring about other's well being, you are cutting off this flow of energy. Simply caring about someone else's well being does not make you more vulnerable to a threat—actually, it makes you more likely to pick up on an actual threat, by being open to a person's subtle energy. You can sense things that you couldn't actually know otherwise and avoid danger. This is being in the Flow.

Compassion is the feeling of love. This can be directed at people or into our actions. Whenever we DO something with love in our hearts, we are infusing it with a special energy that sets it apart from someone doing the same activity without love. It sounds silly to say, but I am certain if you ask yourself, you've experienced this.

Something as simple as going to Starbucks and having the cashier shining brightly as they take your order and hand you your change, as opposed to a cashier who is miserable and doing the exact same job. YOU FEEL IT. It hits you in a visceral way that energizes you . . . or, if you are miserable, hating yourself and the world, it pisses you off, because it is the opposite of the reality you are creating for yourself at that moment.

SELF COMPASSION

Whenever we send negative thoughts or feelings to ourself, we are blocking the flow of Compassion both outwards AND inwards. We are literally cutting ourselves off from this infinite flow of energy and we will be WEAK. Figuring out how to master self compassion is essential for finding more strength.

We need to believe in Ourselves

Most of us have trauma from our childhood that left us with holes in our self-esteem. Whether it was a parent, a sibling, or the kids at school, there were times when you were not loved. And as a child trying to figure out what the heck this whole "Being Human" thing is about, when we didn't feel loved as a kid we filed away the possibility that we weren't WORTHY of love. That we aren't ENOUGH. Good enough, smart enough, successful enough, cool enough . . . it is all about whether we are worthy of love or not, at the root of it.

If we do not feel *good enough* we will struggle to trust ourselves. Trusting ourselves is critical to Spiritual Strength. Without being able to trust ourselves, we will always be susceptible to outside threats to our power and happiness.

And as we've already covered and will continue to hammer home, life is not going to suddenly be smooth, without challenges. Your self-esteem will continue to be challenged up until your last breath—you need to know that you are *good enough* and worthy of love from the inside out. We can't rely on things being all rainbows and sunshine around us to feel like we are good enough. That won't fly.

Focus on deeper truths to keep you centered through tough times, Positive Affirmations, like:

"I am doing my best and I am going to keep on doing my best."
"Practice makes progress."
"Ok, this isn't going as well as I hoped but that means I am learning and getting better at this . . . woo hoo, thanks for the opportunity to grow!!""
(I'm not kidding, I really say this to myself, not in a snarky way!)
"Only I can know what is right for me."

Seriously, whenever things don't go smoothly it is a lesson for growth to be grateful for, not to beat yourself up over. We have to keep resetting that mindset and as we do, it'll get easier. Our mind naturally is in this Ego mode where it is comparing how things are going to our expectations and to how everyone else is doing, to try and get this external, objective sense of whether we are "good enough." Tell it to *zip it*. This way of thinking is torpedoing your strength and your growth. Yes, have goals and yes keep working towards those goals at all costs, but keep your eyes on your own lane as you do your best work . . . know that every day isn't going to be a *win day*, it may be a *learn day*. Both are necessary to achieve greatness.

Believe that with effort and patience you will get better at anything you set your mind to. Science completely backs that up! In Peak: Secrets from the New Science of Expertise, Anders Ericsson cites study after study that shows in *all areas* effort counts twice as much as any "talent" and what seems like "natural talent" can be created with the right sets of practices! So what we used to think about "natural talent" isn't correct at all! We aren't just born with these skills, they take effort! And, with effort, we can all get better at *anything*.

And, at the end of the day, this life isn't personal . . . it is about growth. Your life is a tiny part of something much bigger, and if we remember that we are part of that bigger flow, it keeps us humble. Humility is a key part of self compassion and spiritual strength. Keeping our life in perspective in the bigger picture helps us surrender to the flow of ups and downs that come our way.

Loving ourselves is critical for us to be healthy, but we all know how hard it is. Unfortunately most of us have many subconscious patterns operating that are blocking this self-love. These are called Limiting Beliefs and are the opposite of the positive affirmations we just reviewed. But since so many of these are subconscious, meaning that we aren't even aware of them when they pop up, how can we work to get rid of them?

First, Positive affirmations, literally written anywhere and everywhere that you will see them, seriously works. Keep them simple and use ones that you really consciously believe. If you don't consciously believe them, you need to figure out why you don't believe it before starting to use them and work out those issues . . . for example, if you do not believe that you can get better at anything with practice, you have to crack that nut before using that positive affirmation. If the research and the science don't convince you, you need more help than simple positive affirmations. No shame, just calling it out. Positive affirmations only work if you consciously believe them. There have been studies done demonstrating the effectiveness of using positive affirmations, but also research showing that they backfire if you are using ones that you don't really believe.[3] Believing is key.

When I catch myself limiting myself in any way, I know I have found another opportunity for growth. Anyone who knew me as a young person knows that I am not a naturally *neat* person. My room as a kid literally looked like a bomb went off, and it really didn't bother me. My mom refused to clean up after me, so my room was left to deteriorate until I had no choice but to clean it up. I literally would just make a path on the floor so I could walk from the door to my bed, but otherwise, the entire floor was strewn with clothes, toys, anything that I had out just went somewhere on the floor when I was

---

[3]Psychology Today, Ray Williams, Wired for Success May 2013.

done with it. Of course, my mom didn't encourage this, and there were a lot of fights and shame for me around how messy I was, but I hated to clean and honestly didn't have any natural ability or tendency to be neat. I just was more of an explosive kind of person. Fast forward to me working, and my reviews were always glowing with the exception of, Pam, can you *please* keep your desk neater? It doesn't inspire confidence in your organization skills! But I really just thought that I *couldn't* be neater. I literally thought that I wasn't capable of it.

Fast forward again a bunch more years, me now as a mom, trying to teach my kids to keep an open and positive attitude as they stumbled through challenges. My son Jesse, probably 3 or 4, was doing a lego set that was way beyond his age range and he was getting frustrated. I was in the kitchen, doing the dishes . . . so I called to him, "you can do it buddy, I know it is hard, but don't give up! Even when something is really hard, if you keep a positive attitude, believe in yourself, and just keep trying, you will keep getting better! You may never be the best at something but you can always get better!" And as I called that out to him, I looked down at the dishes that I was begrudgingly washing . . . and I realized that I completely had that block myself with cleaning. I really thought that I *couldn't* clean. And I *hated* to clean. So whenever I *had* to clean (because obviously, it is unavoidable!!!), I would come at it with a horribly negative attitude. I would be saying to myself, "uh, I hate this. I am the worst at this. I can't do this." And obviously, that is ridiculous! I may never be a particularly skilled cleaner, but the idea that I *can't* do it, or I *can't* enjoy it is beyond laughable. I pride myself on being able to enjoy anything! Something doesn't have to *be* fun to *have* fun! So, I realized my block and moved past it. (I'm still not a great cleaner but I am decent and I truly find joy in it, something I never could've imagined.

Compassion and Judgments

Another thing that happens with limiting beliefs: we put them on others. We will talk more about this in depth when we get to Openness and Curiosity, but while we are talking about Compassion let's just quickly hit on judgments. Judging others takes us out of a place of Compassion.

Our brain is literally wired to judge. It is a data processor that is meant to draw conclusions from whatever information that it has available. Those conclusions are then used to take action. The issue is that our mind wants to *be sure* in order to feel safe. This is always an illusion because we can never know *everything* about a situation and ultimately, it doesn't serve us to think that we know, because it makes us much more likely to miss something important.

When all of this comes to Compassion, we can see how our judgments often close us off from caring about others. If we judge someone as "bad" or "unworthy" in some way, we can feel justified in cutting off Compassion.

Remember, Compassion is the flow of energy that connects all parts of the tree, so cutting it off always weakens you, because it cuts you off from your inner flow of energy. If you are still skeptical about that, I get it. Just start experimenting and see how you feel energy wise when you get out of your head and into your heart. Sense how you feel for yourself.

Feelings aside, if we think that we can *know* another person's situation enough to decide if they are good or bad, worthy or unworthy, we are always wrong. There is *always* more to the situation than we can possible see . . . and while there is no part of this that is saying we don't hold people accountable for their behavior, finding Compassion means that we stay open to the things that we cannot know and caring about their well being even when they are behaving destructively.

Thinking that we are better than anyone else is an example of judging, and it can sometimes seemingly disguise itself in kindness: Pity. Pity is literally when we judge another and feel better off than them in that moment, instead of recognizing that we are all equal even in troubling times. If we pity someone, and we decide to be generous with them, that is kindness bourne of judgment and not Compassion. The reality is that we are all equal from a spiritual standpoint. There isn't anyone who has lived that is better than you or worse than you. Our mind of course doesn't see things that way, and there are times when "feeling bad" for someone rises up and we try and do something kind. I will always encourage kind actions, but I need to tell you that pitying anyone carries with it negative energy that will come back to us. So, remember to tell your mind to zip it and go into your heart and feel the equality of the human condition. Then, practice Compassion.

Needing to be right

One of the traps we frequently fall into is the egoic need to be right and how that impacts our Compassion. When it comes to conflict, when someone sees something differently than we do, our ego often gets stuck in the need to be right, and goes into Fight or Flight to defend the perceived threat to the "am I good enough" challenge. We will talk more about embracing the idea of being wrong, not fearing it, but for now, start to think about how often we are confronted with the choice of either needing to be right or being compassionate. When we feel the need to defend what we believe to be right, instead of staying open, we cut off Compassion. Here is what I say to myself when I get stuck: *I do not need to be right. I need to be as Compassionate, Courageous and Wise as I can be.* We can't be as wise as possible with a closed mind. I always know that the possibility exists that I am wrong, and that is ok.

Fragilization

Another common Compassion trap that can occur is fragilization. When we care about someone and want to keep them safe and healthy, we can inadvertently fragilize them. Fragilization is when we treat someone AS IF they were fragile and unable to handle something. We do this with the best of intentions, but it is rooted in a judgment based in fear, and it never serves the person that we care about. They can sense if we think that they are fragile and by treating them as if they are fragile, we are robbing them of the opportunity to get strong. We need to be mindful of the times that we are trying to protect someone, and ask ourselves if we are possibly fragilizing them. We need to commit to anti-fragilization if we want to practice true Compassion. And we need to treat ourselves in the same way, because we can fragilize ourselves just like we can fragilize others.

Compassion and Vulnerability

One of my favorite teachers is Brené Brown. If you haven't read or watched/listened to her, I can't recommend her enough. Her TED Talks on Shame and Vulnerability are simply brilliant and hysterical. She's a research sociologist who has done game changing work in the areas of shame, vulnerability and courage and she's the first person who taught me about the power of vulnerability.

In an interview with the UK based Telegraph, it is described how "she tried first to understand why a handful of people believe in their own worthiness; she calls these people 'Wholehearted'. . . . Is Wholehearted another word for happy, I ask her? 'No,' she says adamantly. 'In fact I think our capacity for Wholeheartedness can never be greater than our willingness to be broken-hearted. It means engaging with the world from a place of vulnerability and worthiness. It's about being all in, saying, "I'm here and I'm going to love you fully and if you cheat on me you're going to devastate me and break my heart, but I'm not holding back because this (life) is short."[4]

The way that Brené Brown describes being "Wholehearted" and its link to vulnerability is powerful because it shines a light on the connection between Compassion and Surrender. You have to cultivate faith or trust that everything (especially you) will be OK in the end, or you will not be able to fully practice Compassion. There is this true sense of vulnerability that needs to be embraced to really go there. That vulnerability is Surrender.

Imperfect Compassion

So listen, we are not Buddha. Compassion isn't easy to master, and when you do, you literally are a Master. So this is going to be messy. There is no way around it. We need to embrace the process as opposed to the result. If something painful comes from your best attempts at being Compassionate, it is an opportunity for growth and part of our higher good. Always.

---

[4]Helena de Bertodano UK Telegraph 17 Sep 2012

It always felt good to me to be kind, and I often wondered as I was working on figuring all of this out for myself, if I liked being kind because of a narcissistic "see, I am a good person" kind of validation. Was it just a cover up for my insecurities? Lord knows I had plenty!

It is hard to untangle *why* it feels good to be kind, but as I've peeled away the layers of what I know to be true and what I realize not to be true, I can tell you that being kind *intrinsically* feels good not just because of the validation of an insecurity about being a good person . . . it feels good to be kind because there is a flow of life that you are a part of, and you are allowing it to flow freely through you without interference. This is a pure energy. We always have an energy flowing through us, and it lights us up when we allow it to pass to another. We shine.

Of course, most people can think of a time when it felt good to be unkind. If someone did something that hurt us, or something we judged as unfair, our instinct will usually be to *get them back*. For me, there were especially times when it felt good to be unkind to myself, when I was so disappointed in myself and was deep in shame. When we hate, either ourselves or others, it feels good to be cruel. It validates the lack of love that our mind believes is true.

If someone hurts us, we can understand why it feels good and instinctive to hurt them back. It seems to be an equal reaction. Our mind thinks that *we* have been wronged, and that this gives us power, because it thinks that we now have something over the person that we are angry with. We have a right to revenge, to be cruel, to make them feel *bad*, because they made us feel *bad*. Our mind can't make sense of releasing that kind of perceived power, which is to say that our mind can't make sense of forgiveness. And therefore our mind cannot heal. It takes getting out of our mind and into our heart to figure out the truth of these wounds . . . and how to heal them.

Forgiveness

This is forgiveness. Forgiveness is always about healing ourselves, and it doesn't have anything to do with approving of what happened or not holding the person accountable. Forgiveness is allowing ourselves to rise above what happened; to not let it weigh us down. Until we forgive, we literally are giving our power to the person or situation that hurt us. While we are still wounded, we are not as powerful as we can be if we figure out how to forgive.

Practicing Forgiveness goes hand in hand with practicing Compassion, because our wounds are what blocks our ability to be compassionate. It is ALWAYS in our best interests to forgive ourselves or others whenever there is a wound, because it is the act of forgiveness that heals. This has nothing to do with doing anything for anyone else, it is literally enabling us to rise up out of the heaviness of the hurt and be healthy again, to take our power back. So as soon as you realize you are hurt by something, take the time to work on forgiveness. This means moving out of your head and into your heart to let go of the wound. It will ALWAYS make you stronger to do this.

Think about a situation where a friend asks you to help them out with a business project but you don't get anything in writing because it is a friend . . . and then your *friend* doesn't compensate you or give you any credit for the work you did. Objectively, a situation that is not in integrity on any level, personal or professional. Anger is completely appropriate in this situation, but does being angry get you anywhere? It may if your *friend* responds to your anger, but what if they don't? If your *friend* won't handle this situation with integrity, there isn't anything that you can actually do. You are stuck in this situation and your brain will probably be equally stuck, mulling over the wound. Your mind gets stuck because it *thinks* that the wound *gives* you power over the other person and/or situation, because it thinks you are *due* something in return because of *the injustice* you endured. And in this case, you are understandably and rightfully due compensation for your work, but if you didn't have anything in writing, you probably won't be able to prove that or get that. So does holding onto this wound give you any power in actuality? No, by holding on to the wound you are staying in a weakened state, and the reality of revenge is always much more messy and costly than the idea of revenge. It isn't ever a gain at the end of the day. Forgiveness is always power. By forgiving, you are releasing the power that the situation has over you, and it no longer can make you angry or upset. You can then rise above it and see it in the big picture. In this case, this friend wasn't really a friend at all, and while a painful lesson, it is important to know who you can trust in your life, and moving the people who you can't trust farther away from you. Getting rid of people in your life that you can't trust or who will bring you down is priceless, so however much this business project cost you, I would say that it was worth it.

Many people get confused about forgiveness versus the repairing of trust. If someone hurts you or lets you down in some way, and you forgive them, that doesn't mean that you don't hold them accountable for what they did, nor does it mean that you allow them close enough to do the same thing again. You can forgive someone without repairing trust. Repairing trust refers to a process where who ever hurt you demonstrates that they understand enough or are sorry enough to make you feel that you can trust them again. You hold them accountable for behavior that was unhealthy. This is vital for a healthy relationship, but there will be times when it cannot happen, and there must be more distance in the relationship than there was before the hurt. This a different process than forgiveness—forgiveness is deeper and universal regardless of whether trust can be re-established. Understanding this difference enables us to feel safe enough to forgive anything, freeing our spirit from the weight of the wound, while knowing that we can do what we need to do to maintain the integrity of our space safely going forward.

Practicing forgiveness is perhaps the most important spiritual strength practice we have, because the wounds that we carry around are precisely what is weighing our spirit down. It is like when we allow something to hurt us, we are giving and/or attaching a piece of ourselves to that situation, and we are not longer whole, or less whole, than we were before. That piece of us stays with that situation and we stay attached to it and it weighs us down, holds us back, and keeps us from being able to fully shine. When we forgive, we are taking our power back, taking those pieces back, cutting those cords that were weighing us down, and we are becoming more whole and more powerful. The more we can forgive and heal our wounds, the lighter and lighter our spirit becomes, and it is easier and easier to keep our spirits high. Keeping a positive attitude gets easier and easier. Life gets easier and easier. We get stronger and more powerful.

Learning *how* to forgive is similar to a process we discuss when we get to Surrender—tuning in and letting go. In the moment of pain, it isn't easy, but with acceptance there is a very real way to maintain our integrity while feeling that pain, as we work on all 5 pillars and building our Spiritual Strength. More detail on that when we get to the chapters on Surrender and Relationships.

Compassionate Non-Attachment

It is also integral to figure out how to be Compassionately Non-Attached. This haunted me for a long time and continues to be a daily practice. I had learned enough about Buddhism and other practical philosophies to know that I needed to figure out how to be non-attached—a concept that is described as a release from desire and consequently suffering . . . but being the caring person that I was, I couldn't for the life of me figure out how I could simultaneously care about someone but not have it bother me if they were suffering! That seemed like not caring! And I knew I needed to care!

I've literally been working on this since I was 17 when it became clear that my boyfriend, Josh, who I loved with all of my heart, had a drug problem. My relationship with Josh was one of the most painful things I have had to go through in my life, and naturally it is what I have grown the most from . . . I couldn't have cared about him more, and seeing him make destructive choices tore me apart. I tried everything I could to help him, but if you have ever had someone in your life with an addiction, you know that it is completely out of your hands. Surrender, which we cover in a few chapters, plays a huge role in this—you basically need to work on Surrender at the same time as you work on Compassion, and that is how you figure out Compassionate Non-attachment. There is truly a beautiful powerful state where you continue to love with all of your heart while being unattached to whether the person is happy or suffering.

This is a good example to look at how to practice Compassion—if we imagine someone who we love dearly suffering and miserable, but there is nothing that we can do to help them. They won't listen to us or they won't follow our advice and it is so painful to watch them suffer. We may need to distance ourselves to protect our own spirits, or as one of my yoga teachers says, "Maintain the Integrity of our Space". As we are in pain, we reach a point where we may need space and or help to face the full experience of the pain, calmly leaning into it instead of going into Fight or Flight in reaction to it. Our pain and fears will guide us as to how we need to navigate the relationship. We may need to instill boundaries to protect ourselves from destructive behavior, while forgiving the person for their behavior and sending love from afar, perhaps prayers that they are able to move towards health while accepting whatever their current situation is (aka Surrender!). Obviously we need to really skillfully face our fears through all of this, and that is where Courage comes into our ability to practice Compassion.

With Josh, I knew I needed to distance myself from him to stay safe and healthy, but I hadn't yet understood how to do this without feeling immense guilt. More on this in the chapter on Relationships when we talk about Compassion without Enabling—it all goes hand in hand. Knowing and trusting yourself enough to stay open hearted yet at a safe distance from anything that isn't safe or healthy. All 5 Pillars work together to make this possible.

Cycle of the Breath

Another huge breakthrough in practicing Compassion was learning the Cycle of the Breath. I first learned about the Cycle of the Breath when I was in yoga teacher training at ISHTA in NYC in 2012 from our teacher Alan Finger. I'll admit it, I was skeptical. He explained how the Cycle of the Breath had the inhale, the exhale, and then pauses between each. He then explained that at each point of the cycle, there were associated inner affects that gave us control over our mind. So, even when we felt like we couldn't control how our mind was behaving, we could control our breathing which would lead to control over our mind.

The first example was that he asked us what we had for breakfast yesterday. He paused and then called on someone—as they answered, he informed us that as he asked the question, each of us inhaled however slightly and paused, as we accessed our memory. It was the pause between the inhale and the exhale where we access our mental processes, judgments and memories.

The next example was imagining that we saw a child fall down, hard, in the street. We'd run to them and bend down to them, asking, are you ok?? And then we'd pause, in the space between the exhale in the inhale, as we waited to see if they were ok. That pause between the exhale and the inhale was where we connected with Compassion.

Being the skeptic that I was, I experimented with this for the next few weeks and I was floored: it was spot on.

I could use this trick to get out of my mind when I was dealing with an unpleasant situation and prone to being critical and judgmental and unempathetic—I'd watch my breathing and keep my attention on the pauses between the exhale and the inhale. I found that this practice lessened my brain's critical diatribe with each round of the breath, and I was able to feel my heart more and more. I got better and better at keeping my heart open and being compassionate and quieting the judgments. This worked wonders on my relationships because the person felt safer and more cared for and was naturally able to respond to me with more Compassion instead of being defensive. How could I not have been taught this before?

More Practice

In addition to what we have covered so far, there are many ways to practice Compassion, to get stronger in rewiring your brain to have Compassion be your default mode. It takes strength to have an open heart and keep it open even through pain, so practice is really, really important. Practice when it's easy to make it easier when it is hard!

Random acts of kindness are one of my favorite ways to practice Compassion. It is like priming the pump, so regardless of how you are feeling, by practicing random acts of kindness it'll get Compassion flowing. You spark it in someone else by your actions, so even if you weren't *feeling* Compassionate, that spark will help re-ignite positivity within you. And if you were already feeling high, it'll give you even more to feel positive about.

I remember one day that I had a rough morning and I was feeling a bit stuck and blue, and I had to walk through Grand Central to get to my office. One of the things that I love about Grand Central is that there's ALWAYS an opportunity to offer to take someone's picture. So, there was this adorable family I think from Italy, a mom, a dad, and three gorgeous kids and I asked if they wanted me to take their picture. They were appreciative and handed me their camera and I took their pic and then handed the camera back and I literally will NEVER forget the look on the little boy's face. He was about Jesse's age at the time, maybe 6, and he was literally BEAMING appreciation and love. I don't know exactly why he was so appreciative, if he thought maybe New Yorkers wouldn't be nice or if he was afraid in general or what, but HIS FACE! I definitely was no longer blue after that face.

Another practice I love is when I am on the subway I notice how beautiful everyone is in their unique way, I look at their eyes and feel their lives, so rich with detail, imagining the people they love and who love them . . . I love them for exactly who they are, even though I don't know them at all. I know it sounds weird but it is really powerful and definitely worth trying!

We will talk more about non-judgment and acceptance in later chapters but they are also wonderful ways to practice Compassion. When someone is imperfect, we have the opportunity to stay in a place of non-judgment, where we do not assign "good or bad" or "right or wrong" and stay loving even in the face of the imperfections. Accepting people for who they are, imperfections and all, and staying loving towards them is something that will pave the way for it to be easier to do as the imperfections (and painful consequences) get more intense.

Ultimately, it is practicing Compassion when it is "easy" that will set us up for being stronger when it is hard.

Self Care

Self Care is a necessary form of practicing Compassion. If we do not maintain the integrity of our space both physically, mentally and spiritually, we are not going to be able to do ANYTHING net positive out in the world. The fundamentals of self care, eating real food, getting good sleep and moving, are non-negotiable. You simply cannot be sustainably healthy without those practices. You will not be able to be your best. I know, we all *know* that—so why is it so hard to do?

I think that the root of why we have such a hard time practicing these fundamentals are the unhealthy issues we are struggling with in other areas of our life. If we aren't secure enough, we won't want to set a digital sunset, turn off our devices, and get a good night sleep because we fear the impact it will have on our job and our security and/or our ego. If we felt secure in our sense of worth and safety, not craving external stimulation to distract us, we'd *go to sleep*. So, like everything we talk about here, it is all about balancing these practices, a little bit at a time in all areas. Get better sleep, work on improving your self esteem and security and the epiphanies that need to happen to surrender what you need to surrender. It all goes hand in hand and I know, it isn't easy.

Eating healthy food for nourishment instead of pleasure—same thing goes. If we are fulfilled in other areas of our life, we won't feel called and attached in the same way as do now to ice cream, chocolate and other comfort foods. Can we enjoy treats at times? Of course. If we really enjoy something and aren't attached to it, which means that we aren't making unhealthy decisions around it, by all means. Have ice cream sometimes. But again, it's about all of this other work at the same time, and it is hard. So maybe no, you can't have ice cream for awhile if it is filling a void or part of a compulsion while you work on rewiring your brain. Only you can know that for yourself.

Exercise! Literally every research study under the sun stresses the power of movement on our mental and physical health—so why do so few people do it? Of course we all want to live as long, healthy lives as possible, so why aren't we exercising? Again, if we were healthy in other ways, practicing Courage to get out of comfort zone, loving our self, being grateful to have a body that is capable of joyful movement, staying Open and Curious to what could come of it, exercise would be easier to make happen.

That is why the inner self-care fundamentals, knowing how your spirits are and honoring whatever you are feeling with care and attention, are so important. If you aren't feeling happy, pay attention to it and figure out what is going on. If you are feeling stressed or anxious or overwhelmed, pay attention to it and figure out what is going on! You need to care for your inner state as much as you need to care for your outer state. It all goes hand in hand.

If Gratitude is the root structure of our Spiritual Strength, Compassion is like the life force itself that is flowing up and out. Connecting with Compassion allows us to be alive and live our life to the fullest extent possible.

COMPASSION BONUS:
Purpose and Greatness

Compassion has a power when it comes to creativity, inspiration and finding deeper meaning in your life. With an open heart for yourself, for others and for life, there is a flow. This flow sparks joy...and creativity and inspiration. You see good and can BE GOOD. You are much more likely to find deep meaning in your life and feel connected to something much bigger than yourself. This is when we start to find it easier to tap into our creativity and the bravery necessary to do our greatest life work. Feeling like you want to have a mission instead of a job. Doing what you do because you LOVE it, not because there is any obligation! Being of service to others without feeling the need to make it *personal* is the path to liberation when it comes to our work. We can get to the point that we do the work because we love doing it, not because we feel obligated or are tied to a result or a reward. Even if that seems too far away from your world right now, there is the simple fact that if we love what we are doing, there is an energy going into our work that inherently takes the quality of the output up significantly. People can tell if you love your work. Doesn't matter if you are a garbage man or a lawyer or an artist . . . if you love what you are doing it shows and it will bring great rewards.

In her recent book, *Grit*, Angela Duckworth shows how effort counts twice in the equation of greatness that we achieve—passion and perseverance are the determining factors of whether we achieve what we set out to achieve.

Her equation:
Talent × Effort = Skill.
Skill × Effort = Achievement

I repeat for emphasis: Effort counts twice.

What makes us not give up, not stop putting in the effort no matter what? Love. Compassion.

Chapter 3

COURAGE

Courage is the most important of all the virtues, because without courage you can't practice any other virtue consistently. You can practice any virtue erratically, but nothing consistently without courage.

—*Maya Angelou*

Courage is facing fear and pain and leaning into it, instead of running away from it or fighting it. Fear will always be a part of being human because pain will always be a part of life. Learning to skillfully navigate fear, as opposed to unskillfully navigating fear (which turns into anxiety) is critical to our inner strength. Cultivating the courage necessary to do this is a fundamental building block in our spiritual strength.

Courage and Pain

Life is painful: both physical and emotional pain are an inescapable fact of life. And at the end of the day, our body is going to break down and we are going to die, and everyone we love is going to die. I know that this is rather blunt, but beating around the bush is in no way helping us live our best lives. And, of course, there are seemingly infinite smaller pain points on a daily basis. Little things like being late, someone speaking to you with disrespect, someone unfairly getting a promotion, a deal falling through... Frequent doses of big pain and little pain is a part of life.

Thanks to our mind's survival instinct, pain = fear. Our mind anticipates possible pain and triggers fear to try and get us to avoid it. Makes perfect sense and it is an awesome system, one that is responsible for us still being here on this planet! Fear is awesome and we are lucky to have it. The problem is that being human these days is not as simple as it was in the days of a cave. Our pain doesn't just stem from putting our hand in the fire and our fears aren't just about a coyote taking our child—our life is much more complex. Yes, we still want to feel safe, but not feeling worthy of love is the root of a lot of our pain.

Plus, past trauma, pain that was unprocessed/unhealed, continues to trigger fear long after our conscious memory of the event fades. Adding all of that past trauma on top of our current insecurities, and we have a lot of pain and fear to face every day.

Hidden Weaknesses in our Courage

I probably don't need to convince you of the power of Courage, but I want to draw your attention to examples of when we might be missing Courage and not even knowing it.

You get angry. You act out of that place of anger. You look back and see that you made a mess of things.

Are you wondering what that has to do with Courage? Anger is *always* a cover up for sadness, pain or fear.[5] Without Courage, we can't face the pain or fear that is the root of the issue at hand. And we can't shift from destructive behavior that ultimately brings more pain to constructive behavior that ultimately brings more joy.

Last week when we were in Colorado, my 8 year old son, Jesse, and 11 year old daughter, Talia, were playing outside with my 5 year old nephew, Olin. Olin threw a snowball and pegged Jesse square in the face. It definitely hurt Jesse, and then Talia laughed. Jesse was enraged, turned to Talia and attacked her, fists flying to her chest. Jesse normally is gentle and kind to his sister, but the physical pain of the snowball combined with the emotional pain of the laugh sparked destructive behavior.

We've all seen moments like this.

Physical pain triggers our Fight and Flight reflex powerfully fast. It overrides the part of our brain that keeps us considerate and mindful. The same thing goes for emotional pain such as humiliation. It takes both awareness and Courage to avoid the destructive outbursts that our Fight and Flight reflex can inappropriately spark.

---

[5]Leon Seltzer, PhD, Psychology Today July 2008, What Your Anger May be Hiding.

If you are a parent and were ever bitten or hit hard by your child, you know what I mean. Despite your love for your child, in that moment the reflex isn't in line with the gentle compassion we normally cultivate for our children. I remember Talia coming up behind me as a toddler and biting the back of my leg. I almost kicked her across the room, barely catching myself with a deep breath before scooping her up and sternly saying NO!

Emotional pain is the same. Grief, shame, embarrassment and fear are triggers that send us into a reflexive Fight or Flight position. Skillfully navigating those emotions with Courage is the key to making our situation better, instead of worse.

We will do a deeper dive on all of this in later chapters, but here's the deal: Shame, Guilt, Apathy, Anger, Desire and Pride all require practicing Courage to move out of the negative, destructive behavior zone into a positive place. We need to bravely face and lean into the pain in order to avoid *acting out of the pain*. If we act out of any of these states, without bravely owning our feelings and looking at what is really going on within ourselves, *and what needs to heal*, we are making our situation worse... whether we can see it or not.

Getting close to any of these feelings is *super* uncomfortable. In the case of emotional pain, deep guilt and shame or grief, it seems instinctively unbearable to face. So whenever these feelings get triggered, our mind is automatically saying *move away*—distract! blame others! Do Not Go Here! Our Ego really doesn't want to experience the vulnerability that getting close to these feelings entails. The reality is, though, getting all up in these emotions is the only way to heal them, aka make our lives better as opposed to worse. And we cannot do this without Courage.

The same goes for the countless smaller triggers that cause us irritation and anger in our day to day lives—if we just allow the triggers to send us into the reactive, unmindful Fight or Flight mode where we act without Compassion, we will consistently be making our situation worse. We need to bravely and skillfully navigate what is being triggers. More specifics on *how* coming up.

Authenticity

Another thing we can't do without courage: Be Authentic. We are all unique snowflakes, aren't we? Each of us weird in our own way, and if we are looking outside of ourselves for that external validation of whether we are good enough or whether we are on the right track, we are never going to be able to be ourselves. No one can know how to be you except you. And, in being you, you will be different, and there will be people who are going to hate, judge, criticize, not see what you see... so you will need to be brave as hell to follow your own inner vision for *being you*. And if it isn't obvious, if you aren't being Authentic, you aren't tapping into your highest power. There is only one of you, you are it, and you are it for a reason. You are meant to do something great with your life, and I have seen how crazy forces will come to our aid when we are bravely living our truth. But if you aren't being you, if you are looking externally for validation and feedback and wavering on who you are, you aren't going to be Spiritually Strong.

It is incredibly common in our society for people to be inauthentic—to say and do things that they think will win them favor from others, instead of what feels right or true to them on a deeper level. To "like" people for what they can do for them, instead of there being an genuine respect and appreciation for who they are as people. Perhaps without even being aware of it. This stems from insecurity and as all 5 pillars are practiced, one will find less and less of a propensity to engage in this type of inauthenticity.

Honesty and Integrity

And there are times that it is so hard to be honest, to say what we need to say, to follow our hearts even if it hurts someone else. Being honest is critical to having Spiritual Strength, because if our head and our heart are out of alignment we are going to be pulled in two different directions. Talk about diluting strength and power. We have to get ourselves together!

Brené Brown defined Integrity as: Choosing Courage over Comfort; Choosing what is Right over what is Fun, Fast or Easy; and Choosing to Practice our Values over simply Professing them.[6]

---

[6]Brene Brown, Rising Strong (Spiegel & Grau; August 25, 2015)

Hell Yeah. I choose Courage.

If we do not live our values, our head and our heart will be out of alignment and you will literally be selling yourself out, giving your power away to something that is not in your highest good. And you will know it and feel it and until you forgive yourself (which, as we already have covered, do as soon as possible) it will be weighing you down. The more often you choose what is right over what is easy, the lighter and happier and stronger you will be.

So how can we practice and cultivate our Courage?

First, understanding fear is key. When we get hit with fear, we immediately go into Fight or Flight. As the name implies, Anger, Blame, Escapism are signs that you are in Fight or Flight. Fear is literally hardwired—it has to act fast in order to facilitate our survival, and it is part of our autonomic nervous system... so the split second we get a jolt of fear, our entire chemical nervous system goes into full effect. - this is what we call Fight or Flight or our Sympathetic Nervous System. There are two neurological pathways involved in Fight or Flight—we can think of the pathways in our brain like a "low road" and a "high road".[7] The "low road" involves the pathway from our five senses directly to our amygdala which releases the adrenalin right away. The "high road" runs almost simultaneously to our cortical center which can use reason to determine

---

[7]Dr. Seth Norrholm, PhD uses this terminology

if there is an actual threat. Depending on the maturity of the brain (this "high road" develops during childhood and gets more sophisticated as intelligence develops), the "high road" may override the "low road"—for example, you are walking down the street and all of a sudden a dog leaps out from behind the bush at you, and your "low road" response gives you a shot of adrenaline, but then your "high road" response looks through everything that you know and you recognize that it's your neighbor's dog who actually is a love muffin, so you don't need to be afraid of it.

We have all experienced moments like this, when we get frightened but then we realize we have nothing to be afraid of. That is the two "roads" of our mind's fear response at work. Unfortunately, the "high road" doesn't always end up being used as often or as effectively as it could be, and this is where things go haywire.

Let's be super clear—it goes without saying that fear has served humanity well—we wouldn't still be here without fear and the Sympathetic Fight or Flight response. The problem, however, is that our brain hasn't evolved as quickly as our lives have—our lives no longer revolve around matters of survival on a daily basis the way they did when we were living in primitive times. We aren't out hunting and foraging and having to physically defend our lives the way humans did way back when. Our lives are much SAFER now on a daily basis, but the threats that we perceive are more complicated. Simple physical threats used to be what caused our fear—now, our lives are fraught with fears around feeling pain of any kind, physical and emotional, on top of just fear of survival. Things have gotten pretty complicated. Which is great, because it is all about having the opportunity to evolve! If we are busy fighting for survival all day, we can't be concerned with creativity, right? So all of this really is an opportunity for greatness—we just need to figure it out.

Skillfully Navigating Fear

As soon as we are aware that we are feeling fear, we want to start skillfully dealing with it, as opposed to unskillfully reacting to it. When we do not use any skills to navigate our fear, we can end up wasting a huge amount of energy and making destructive decisions. From a neurological standpoint, what happens is that our lower brain activates around a potential threat and then for whatever reason our higher brain doesn't function properly to provide an override where there isn't an actual threat. We stay in Fight or Flight and start going down a road that isn't in alignment with reality... and ultimately, that never ends well.

First, we always need to start by respecting fear. If there is an urgent physical threat, by all means, go into Fight or Flight and protect yourself and your loved ones. If, however, there isn't an actual immediate impending physical threat, being in Fight or Flight mode is not your best move. When we go into Fight or Flight, there is a hormonal response that sends blood to our extremities so we can physically do what we need to do to protect our body and our mind goes into primal, lower thinking mode. We literally get dumber when it comes to any kind of critical thinking.

If we don't actually have a physical threat to fight or run from, all of that extra energy that our body just produced has to go somewhere, so for most of us, it goes into our mind. Our mind will then be very busy making up stories about what it is that we may have to fear. And on and on our mind will go, continually looking for more possibilities to try and avoid whatever it is that we fear, in the meantime, creating *even more fear!* Out of, potentially, nothing. A lot of wasted energy and a lot of opportunity to mishandle situations.

Skillfully dealing with fear, on the other hand, means that you figuratively and/or literally get as close as possible, safely and respectfully, to what it is triggering your fear, so you can determine what actual threat may exist. You respect whatever it is that your mind thinks is posing a danger to ensure you are super smart and safe, and you respect the fear because it is a hugely important tool that we have to help us stay alive. Once you feel fear, you can thank it and take it from there skillfully with your higher brain.

Here's an example to illustrate the difference between skillful fear and unskillful fear: two years ago we moved from NYC to Bronxville, and I was lucky enough to have a house again! One of the first nights my husband was traveling and I was home alone with the kids asleep, I heard a huge bang downstairs—it legit scared the hell out of me. Fortunately, I practice mindfulness these days and brought my attention to my breath to stay calm and quieted my mind. I carefully went downstairs and investigated and found that one of the blinds in the kitchen had come crashing down. Ok, no big deal. I went back to bed.

But I can remember clear as day being a teenager babysitting and being alone at night in big old farmhouses and hearing weird noises and driving myself half crazy fully imagining not only plausible scary reasons for the noises (burglars!), but fully straight out of Stephen King, evil clowns and vampires, and literally got myself so scared that I had to call my dad to have him talk me back down! Clearly, unskillful fear.

So back to present day, if I am not practicing mindfulness, my mind starts going a mile a minute in all of the possible imaginary scenarios of what caused the bang downstairs, and I get more and more frightened... perhaps I get myself so worked up that I can't even get myself to go down and look to see what could've made the noise. Maybe I even have to call my dad in the middle of the night and wake him up to ask for his help to make sure everything is ok!! This is unskillfully dealing with fear.

Obviously, skillfully dealing with fear requires skills (hence the name, "skillfully"!) so here are a few suggestions to try:

First, breathe. We already talked a bit about the Cycle of the Breath, and it is on the inhale that we get confidence. Use that to cultivate your courage. Take long, even, deep breaths in and faster breaths out. We instinctively take a big breathe in for confidence when we are scared, but often we instinctively hold it in! That works against you—you need to keep breathing to skillfully navigate fear. The exhale is where we release toxic energy, and that we definitely want to keep doing that. Even inhales and exhales keep our mind as calm and clear as possible. And, we want to keep our breath steady to keep oxygen rich blood flowing to our brain! So, make sure you aren't holding your breath.

Second, quiet your mind of negative fantasy self talk. It is much harder to be brave when your mind is telling a horrible narrative of the awful outcome of the thing you fear. Shut your mind down saying something like, I don't know what will happen, more shall be revealed. Or, thinking of positive, safe alternatives to explain the situation instead of the negative scenarios. Your mind can only hold one thought in it at a time so discard negative ones and replace with positive ones. Keep doing this as often as possible and you will be rewiring your brain. Seek out times to play with this when it is easy, so when I gets harder, you have the pathway paved.

Simple positive affirmations, like: I can do this. I am strong enough. I am good enough. I can be brave. Believing that you can do it and that things will be ok is the root power behind bravery. *What you believe you will achieve.* Research shows that your body doesn't know when your mind is kidding, so simply saying the positive affirmations in that moment makes a difference, because your body will start to respond as if it were true (yay, brain chemistry!).[8] Just like smiling releases the "happy" hormones, so smile no matter what.[9]

Our minds are also wired to notice and stick on negative possibilities more intensely than positive ones. Another reason why avoiding complaints is so important. Researchers such as Dr. Rick Hanson, a psychologist and New York Times best-selling author, call this the "Negativity Bias"—we are hardwired to notice any negatives or potential threats much more intensely than any positive opportunities. It is simply a survival mechanism. If we know that about our mind and stay aware of our thoughts, we can ask more questions and then benefit from a clearer assessment of the situation.

Anxiety

We can't talk about Courage without addressing anxiety. Anxiety is when our fears become compulsive and end up being in a chronic, automatic, often subconcious and unskillful state. We can feel anxious sometimes or all the time, depending on how bad it gets, and this feeling isn't associated with a specific threat. It also means that we are hypersensitive to perceived threats and have excessive fear responses to those threats.

This happens to us because of our life experiences. Some people are more predisposed to have anxiety than

[8]http://www.huffingtonpost.com/2015/04/16/self-affirmations-boost-performance_n_7079350.html
[9]www.theatlantic.com/health/archive/2012/07/study-forcing-a-smile-genuinely-decreases-stress/260513/

others, but our society now includes overwhelming stimulation and information, with less rest and relaxation time. I suspect most people susceptible to developing anxiety in today's age. Indeed, there is a "Normal" level of anxiety according to the APA[10] and it becomes a disorder when it impacts how you function in your life. Knowing what I know now, just because everyone has something, which makes it normal, does not mean it is okay! There is no reason why we have to experience anxiety in the least. Is it typical and normal for humans in our society? Yes, absolutely, and I will stand on the mountaintop and scream that this isn't *okay* from now until the end of my days. Anxiety is a symptom of something really dysfunctional in our society and I want to see it healed. This is one of the reasons why I am writing this book.

I was in my early 20s when my seemingly silent and/or "normal"anxiety reached a head, as I was hanging out in my LA apartment watching TV as my boyfriend was at band practice. I was as relaxed as I ever could be and all of a sudden I had a shooting pain down the left side of my body. It scared me and I became convinced that something was horribly, physically wrong. I called my poor mom, back in NY, and woke her up and described what I was experiencing which of course had now escalated in my barely being able to breathe. Poor thing stayed on the phone with me while I waited for the ambulance... and then I insisted something was wrong

---

[10]1. American Psychiatric Association. (2013). *The Diagnostic and Statistical Manual of Mental Disorders: DSM 5.*

and they had to take me to the hospital as they were all pretty convinced I was "just having an anxiety attack."

Talk about embarrassing, humbling and expensive... many doctors' appointments later, I was indeed given a clean bill of health. I also now had a commitment to figuring out what the hell I needed to do to address this diagnosis of anxiety.

All of this takes us back to the self care that we talked about—we need to give our bodies and our minds time to rest and recover. We need to respect that miracle that our body is and that our mind is and we need to use our body and our mind in a sustainable way. If we overuse or misuse our body or mind, we are going to run into trouble. Not just anxiety or other mental illnesses, but physical illness as well.

Anxiety is like an overuse injury that we get when we are training for a marathon—if we don't get enough rest, if we don't give our body everything that it needs in between training, we are going to get injured and have a dysfunction. We won't be strong! Needing rest isn't weak, it is a required piece of being strong.

All of the fundamentals of self care, eating real food, getting good sleep, moving, apply when we are talking about anxiety... as do the inner self-care fundamentals, knowing how your spirits are and honoring whatever you are feeling with care and attention. We cannot be strong without the proper care, no matter how awesome we are. Fortunately, there are tools you can use to help.

Power Postures

Amy Cuddy, a Social Psychologist at Harvard Business School talks about the power of posture in her book, *Presence*. Even if you aren't feeling confident, standing or sitting in certain "Power Poses" has been proven to increase your overall confidence level—think, hands on hips like Wonder Woman, and you've got one. You can check out her Ted Talk[11] or book for more.

Dialectical Behavioral Therapy (DBT) Skills

I was lucky enough to spend two years with The Beacon Program, a food and weight program in New York City founded by Molly Carmel. The program is largely based on Dialectical Behavioral Therapy, a type of Behavioral Therapy with four areas of skills to help break the cycle of dysfunctional thinking *leading* to dysfunctional behavior... *that then reinforces* more dysfunction thinking: Mindfulness Skills, Distress Tolerance Skills, Emotional Regulation Skills and Interpersonal Skills. All of these areas of skillfulness support our skillful navigation of fear.

Mindfulness

Mindfulness is being aware of where you are putting your attention—the opposite of this is being in an

---

[11]https://www.ted.com/talks/amy_cuddy_your_body_language_shapes_who_you_are

automatic fog of sorts, where you bounce around following whatever your mind seems to catch on, without any conscious awareness or control. As you practice mindfulness, you are strengthening the cognitive functioning necessary to be in control of your attention and to remain aware of your attention. Being aware of and in control of what we pay attention to is a huge game changer. This gives us the space to respond to what is going on around us as opposed to being stuck in a reactive state, without being able to access the higher parts of our brain to make our best choices.

The emphasis on mindfulness is what originally drew me to Beacon. I already had an established meditation practice and knew how life changing becoming more mindful is. Practicing mediation is the most effective way of building this part of our brain power, but you can practice mindfulness in a multitude of ways. Everything from coloring books to going for a walk... There are mindfulness apps that will ping you to remind you to practice, and you can literally practice as you go about your day. Just search on your phone and you will find many options.

This can be applied literally to any activity, but here is an example of a walking mindfulness meditation (and yes, there is an app for this, too!): Head out for a walk, and start by feeling how your body feels as you walk. If any thoughts come, allow them to drift away and come back to what you are noticing, without judgment or association. Scan your body, first noticing your feet and the sensations as you step and lift each foot, then coming up your legs, feeling how your muscles feel as they flex and release, feel your hips as they hinge back and forth, feel how your abdominals feel as they stabilize the motion, feel how your shoulders sway, feel any tension in your shoulders and neck and notice how you can release that, feel your arms and hands, feel how your face feels if there is a breeze or sun... you see how this can go. And that is just the sense of touch! Next notice what you see, paying attention to each sight, as detailed as possible in all ways, keep scanning and noticing. Again, if any thoughts come, allow them to drift away and come back to what you are noticing, without judgment or association. After focusing on what you see, take your attention to what you hear and repeat the process. It is amazing all that you can hear that you normally don't even notice! This is such a cool practice, it will really change your energy and recenter you, and the more you do it, the more you get better at it, and the more it will lead to being mindful when you aren't specifically setting aside time to practice. This practice is critical to our awareness of our fear response and our ability to skillfully navigate our fear.

Other DBT Areas of Skillfulness

There are so many brilliant, effective skills from DBT in the areas of Distress Tolerance, Emotional Regulation and Interpersonal Effectiveness, and I want to clarify why these are areas that are so critical to be skillful.

We already covered the importance of skillfully handling fear—fear pops up in both Distress Tolerance (the acceptance of whatever painful/scary is happening) and Emotional Regulation (once we feel fearful, how do we regulate that to stay calm aka find Courage in the face of feeling fearful).

Interpersonal Effectiveness is all about how skillfully we navigate our relationships—with these areas of focus[12]:

- Use skills to maintain/improve your relationships
- Use skills to get what you want and need, balancing wants and shoulds, priorities and demands.
- Use skills to build a sense of mastery and self-respect.

We can see how becoming more skillful in those areas will serve to help us feel more secure—helping to stabilize and heal an important area in our lives where we experience destabilization and fear. If we become more skillful in maintaining healthy relationships, we will have real connections to something bigger than ourselves, and have more support in feeling worthy of love. This is huge in cultivating Courage.

The specific skills you learn in a DBT program are online for easy reference and I highly recommend that you check them out and/or seek out a therapist that specializes in DBT.

---

[12]Marsha M. Linehan, DBT Skills Training Manual (Guilford Publications, Inc.: 2014)

There is one other skill in particular that I want to mention from DBT: the THINK Skill—when stuck in Fight or Flight, or you feel stuck in anger, this is one of my favorite skills to get unstuck:

Think about it from another perspective
Have Empathy
Interpretations—come up with lots of different situations that would explain what is happening
Notice—positives about the situation
Kindness—Always be kind in how you handle the situation

It takes mindfulness to remember to practice skills, so the more we practice mindfulness day in and day out, when it is easy, the more you will have the presence to use skills when it is hard.

Be Aware of External Validation

Another practice is to catch ourselves when we are seeking external validation instead of trusting our inner knowing. Remember, you are the only person who knows what is right for you. No one else can tell you what is the right choice for you, if you are meant to be in your job, or in that relationship, or staying or going. You need to be in touch with your inner vibe, what sparks joy vs. what is stressful... Good discomfort (all the magic happens outside of your comfort zone!) vs. stress telling you something is out of alignment. You have to take the time to figure out what you KNOW about yourself without looking around for other people's answers. If you are looking around, you will end up missing your life.

No Avoiding Pain

All of the inner strength in the world will not protect us from pain. And, pain (discomfort) is the touchstone to growth, so believe me when I say that it is a positive force in our lives! You will learn how to move through pain easier and faster by practicing all of this, so it is worth it. If we live in fear of death, pain, or our fears, we are surviving but we will not thrive. We need to ask ourselves where we truly are in our evolution and what we are willing to sacrifice in order to merely try and stay safe? There is a big, beautiful, reasonable middle path that we can live in, leaning into our fear with Courage while respecting all that our fear is teaching us. Not just surviving, but thriving.

Courage alone is quite powerful—someone can be brave without being grateful or connecting with Compassion. However, without Gratitude, Courage will not be rooted. Without Compassion, Courage will not necessarily be positive. Plenty of horrific acts of human history have been perpetuated by brave, misguided men. Point being, Courage alone will not serve us. Just as Compassion without Courage will not serve us. We must work on all of these AT ONCE.

My dad pointed out that it is like a beautifully executed dance—what a disaster if I only focus on my feet! I need to simultaneously direct my arms and hands, listen to and anticipate the music, and bravely move into the next move trusting myself to stay well balanced. My dad is a drummer, so he could've also easily used a drumming analogy... all of life is like that—there is nothing that exists in a vacuum. It is all interconnected.

COURAGE BONUS: Knowing Our Shadow

Courage is the key to going into our pain, and this is what we need to do to heal. Facing our pain, re-living our pain, accepting our pain, moving THROUGH our pain instead of pushing it down, avoiding it, off-loading it. We can't be honest with ourselves and really know ourselves without Courage. We need to face our pain, our shame, our anger, our wounds and love all of that as much as we love our positive sides. Our shadow isn't "bad", it is simply unknown—so having the Courage to go there no matter what we find about ourselves is the path to liberation. We will no longer have anything to fear about ourselves. Our shadow isn't bad in any way, it is simply unknown.

Chapter 4

SURRENDER

Surrendering to the ebb and flow of the ocean is what allows us to surf the waves.

—- *Pamela Palladino Gold*

Surrender is a tough word for a lot people. It brings to mind failure or loss or giving up—concepts that seem quite negative, undesirable, and ill-advised. After all, we are all about achieving our goals, and as everyone knows, we can't be successful reaching our goals if we give up when the going gets tough. So it is really important to explain what we are talking about when we use the word Surrender.

There is this big, beautiful middle path when it comes to living life, where you are doing your best in each moment and at the same time Surrendering to the flow of what is and what comes next. Surrendering to what is yet to be revealed in the face of giving everything your all. Then, it's the next moment, where things are however they are, and you again do your best. This is the process of living in the moment. Surrender is directed to the part of life that is ultimately out of your control, while still committing to giving 150% to everything that IS in your control. Surrender is accepting the fact that a tremendous amount of life is out of our control, and as long as we are doing our best, whatever happens, we are going to just keep doing our best and accepting what comes next. No attachments to results, or expectations on outcome. Continually looking at whatever is and saying to yourself, ok this is how it is, so it must be exactly as it is meant to be in this moment . . . so now, how can I make it better?

Surrender is the toughest of the 5 pillars for me and I think for most people. It requires trust in something that you can't see or make sense of with your mind alone. With so much at stake, that is really hard.

Radical Acceptance

Tara Brach's brilliant book, *Radical Acceptance,* is all about Surrender. If we spend our energy fighting what IS, it is a waste of energy and keeps us unclear about what to do next. We won't be able to create positive change. It is so important to understand that acceptance isn't *approval*—this is where a lot of people get stuck. You can absolutely accept the reality of a situation without approving of it. Acceptance is committing to fully embracing reality—no matter how painful, undesirable or challenging. This is essential in order to be able to make the best move forward. This is a skill that is critical in the mundane, day to day of normal life, as well as in the big moments of challenge.

I was at the Bleecker Street Playground one Spring day with my husband, Roger, and the kids. We were working on selling our apartment so I was sitting at a picnic table by the climbing structure, emailing with our realtor, while Roger was over at the swings with the kids. A little girl fell pretty hard off of the play structure in front of me, about 8 feet away, and the mom started screaming that she couldn't breath. I ran over to support her, and was telling her that she probably just had the wind knocked out of her—that had happened to Talia the year prior and it was super scary until she started to breath again (in Talia's case, she also had hit her head hard and had blood coming out of her mouth, so I had called 911—that was a fun day). But the mom continued to scream and added that she was choking, so I said, "OK then we need to do the Heimlich." The mom continued to literally scream and didn't move so I grabbed the little girl and began giving her the Heimlich. She still wasn't breathing after about 10 thrusts so I flipped her over on my lap and tried the shoulder thrusts. Still not breathing after 10 thrusts on her back, but conscious, I got her upright again and tried more of the Heimlich thrusts. You can imagine how I was feeling at this point—we were in the middle of a large group of people and I started to yell to see if there was anyone else qualified to help me. I am CPR trained thanks to my personal training certification but I am not a doctor or a nurse. I've never actually had to do this before. This little girl had not been breathing for awhile at this point and I had to face the reality of the situation.

I was completely terrified that this little girl was going to die in my arms. Someone else came over to help right as the little girl started to breathe again—it turned out that it had been a rice krispy treat she had been eating as climbing on the play structure.

If I hadn't surrendered to the situation, I would've wasted time and energy avoiding taking on the role that I found myself in. I definitely didn't want to be responsible for that little girl's life. No way, no how. I had never been in a situation like that before and I hope to never be again. Fighting with the mom or trying to find someone else before helping would clearly not have been the right thing to do. But believe me, if I had felt like there were any choice, I would not have wanted to be the person responsible for that little girl's life.

The key takeaway from that day on the playground is "It Is What It Is". Sometimes, many times, we find ourselves in situations that we never would have chosen, and that we have to lean in to whatever is the case in the present moment, embracing it...however uncomfortable, scary, undesirable or "unfair". That is Radical Acceptance. And then we can see clearly and calmly what our next best move is. We can act our *best* and have our best shot for the next moment being on the best path.

Openness and Surrender

Our fifth pillar of Openness and Curiosity goes hand in hand with Surrender because you need to stay Open in order to continue to Surrender. Part of the problem with being human is that our minds are really limited in their perceptions and analysis of situations. Our minds are constantly wanting to judge situations as "good" or "bad" and close down/ pull away if it is judged negatively. But things can seem "bad" at times and later we look back and realize how it was actually in our best interests how it all played out. We just never know what is going to happen next. Of course our mind desperately wants to judge the situation to try and feel safe, and Surrender and Openness flies in the face of that need to feel safe. It obviously takes a lot of Courage to be able to let go like that.

I will never forget one of my favorite yoga teachers, Ali Cramer, saying in class, "that moment when you realize that everything isn't in your control is either the scariest or the most liberating moment of your life." That is Surrender, and it can be terrifying.

When to Practice Surrender

So, how can we practice Surrender? How can we make it easier? First, let's talk about the WHEN.

Being aware of when we start to fight what IS instead of Surrendering to what is out of our control is actually pretty easy once you learn to connect the dots to what it feels like. And here is what it feels like: Stress. Yup. *Any form of stress* is a sign of a need to Surrender. Stress means that you are identifying with something that isn't true for you, and trying to make it true . . . and Surrender is the answer.

So let's pick a stressful situation, any stressful situation. I happen to be on an airplane right now, and I think that many people would agree that in general, air travel is stressful. Especially these days with the long security lines and if you happen to have small children. Flights get delayed, cancelled, vacations get ruined. So, let's look at that stress: suppose hypothetically that you hit worse than expected traffic, arrive just an hour before take off, and there is a line a mile long curbside to check the bags. If you are solo, maybe you go look inside and see that the line is even longer, so return to the outside line. There's like, literally 40 people in front of you and now you've got 50 minutes until your plane is set to go. How are you feeling about now? I'd bet stressed. Here's the trick: by Surrendering to what is out of your control and shutting down the false narrative that your mind is firing off that isn't serving you in the least (YOU ARE GOING TO MISS YOUR FLIGHT!), first of all, because it's not true, but even if it were, it hasn't happened yet so it doesn't matter - you've got to stay present and remember, "what you believe you achieve", so don't go believing negative prophecies! But Surrendering to the fact that there is a hell-of-a-long line and you've got very little time to solve this problem, and Surrendering that, despite how sure your mind is, you actually have no idea what will happen next (yay for Openness!) you will re-center yourself, get clear and start seeing possible solutions to act on. Like grabbing a porter or someone who works there and telling them really nicely that you've got a tight flight. There's a much better chance that people will help if they feel your positive energy.

The good news is that you can start to practice this, as with the other pillars, when it is easy. You don't need to wait until you are stressed to start. You can play with this in traffic when you aren't in a rush, because it is easier to practice Surrender when less is at stake. But that practice is just as important as when it is hard. It is just vital to recognize and remember that whenever you are aware that you're feeling stress, practicing Surrender would definitely help you. I can hear you now, because I would've been saying the same thing a few years ago . . . Are you kidding me? I'm already stressed out thanks to an insanely challenging situation, and you are telling me to Surrender?!

I can imagine that your mind thinks that this is completely ridiculous (not to mention irritating), because your mind thinks *stress* means "work even harder" or "I am already overwhelmed and now you want me to add on something else?!? I've got too much on my plate in those moments as it is, by definition!" Yes, I want you to practice mindfulness in the face of all stress. This will help you figure out what you need to Surrender. Stress = time to practice your skills. *Especially* when you feel stressed. And, I want you to get excited about it, because it's life changing.

Here's another example: it was a typical weekday, I was getting home with the kids after school. We leave our house all together at 7:20am and head into the city, kids get dropped at school, then I head to my office until it is time to pick them back up and then we head back home. So, our house is left in a rush in the morning, needless to say, so it is left in quite a state . . .

This particular day, it was a Thursday and the kids had after school, so we weren't getting home until after 630pm. Upon getting home, I had to help the kids get going on their homework, get dinner made, get the laundry done, take out the garbage and recycling . . . so I knew getting home I had a lot on my plate.

Upon walking into our kitchen, I was greeted by an overflowing mound of gross dishes in the sink. I felt this overwhelm and despair wash over me and I could tell I was moving towards losing it. But, thanks to my practices, I took a deep breath and asked myself what part of me was freaking out, and I knew the answer: the part of me that thinks that if I don't have a clean house, well-fed kids, etc. etc. that I am not good enough. I'm not a good enough mom, good enough wife etc. etc. I could then take a moment to laugh at myself and release that silly idea and surrender to whatever I was going to be able to get done in that next hour. And what didn't get done, didn't get done. The earth would continue to spin. It didn't define me as a mom, wife or person in any way. And that Surrender freed up a crazy amount of energy with which I somehow got *everything* done in literally what felt like a blink of an eye. (It was literally about 15 minutes and I had somehow accomplished everything that needed to get accomplished)

It is counter-intuitive (or counter reason, because our intuition actually knows this, it is our mind that is slow to catch on), but the more you let go, the more life force/ positive energy will come to your aid. It's like we've become constrictors, tightly wound around our lives, cutting off the flow of possibilities and greatness . . . the stress, the fighting to stay in control, it literally cuts off our life force.

By fighting what is, and trying to control what comes, with great urgency and expectation (heaven forbid things don't go the way we plan!), we waste all of this energy that we *could* be using for positive synergy, noticing and capitalizing on opportunities we miss because we are stuck in negative control mode. We miss the opportunities inherent in the unexpected outcomes because we are so disappointed or distraught it didn't go the way we expected. We resist and then attach, resist and attach . . . instead of flowing.

So HOW? How do you loosen that white-knuckled death grip on the flow of your life?

We already talked about how Courage and Surrender go hand in hand. It takes Courage to Surrender. Gratitude goes hand in hand with Surrender as well, because if we stay rooted in Gratitude, we literally take whatever comes as a blessing even if it is undesirable, keeping us clear headed and flowing. And remember, it takes Surrender to feel Grateful in the face of pain or unfulfilled goals. They are interlocked—you need to practice them both at the same time. So practicing Courage (refer back to the skills like positive affirmations) and Gratitude are both integral in the practice of Surrender. We also talked about staying Open to the things that have yet to happen - there is no such thing as a sure thing, so no matter how unlikely a positive outcome may seem, believe that it could happen. Repeat after me, "I believe in miracles" or, if you prefer "it ain't over 'til it's over."

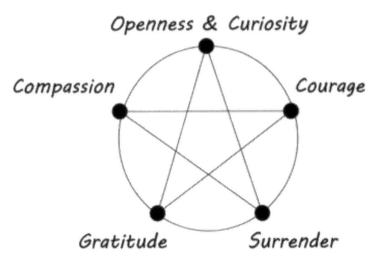

Mindfulness

I know it isn't easy or natural to be mindful of our stress. In her book, *Rising Strong*, Brené Brown pointed out that people tend to fall into one of two modes when it comes to their stress response. We are either over-controlling or we withdraw. It is super important to be aware of that tendency, remember it, and be sensitive to that in ourselves and others. There is zero question that I become over controlling. Before I figured all of this out, if I started to feel stress I would launch into "I've got this" mode and get extremely bossy, intolerant and super high energy in trying to avoid whatever it was that I was afraid of. Classic example, I used to get really triggered by the possibility of being late to anything. All of my life, being late equaled being rude and not good enough. I have been on the receiving end of people being late and seemingly unaware of the impact that it had on others and there was no way that this was ever going to be me. So, at any situation that could possibly lead to me being late, which in my life is about 6 times a day, I would ramp up to stressed, over controlling fight mode. The fight was "I cannot be late"—and of course, I could be late. There may be consequences to being late that were undesirable, but I could very well be late. And, it would be ok. It wouldn't be a life or death situation. But ugh, until I figured this out I was a pill to be around.

My brother, on the other hand, withdraws when things get stressed and unpleasant. He doesn't go into the over controlling b*tch mode, but he may go into "I don't care" mode, or angry "get away from me and leave me alone mode".

Knowing which category you and your loved ones fall into on their stress response is helpful because you can mindfully catch yourself and it helps you be more supportive of your loved ones when they need it . . . and it helps you not take their behavior personally.

And then, there is meditation. A meditation practice gives you the power to untangle your attention away from getting swept up in the whirlpool of stress, and instead pay attention to how you are feeling and using your skills to navigate the moment with the grace of Surrender and clarity. Meditation helps us know the difference instinctively between what we can control and what we can't, so we can surf the wave of life with grace, giving everything within our control our ALL while not wasting any energy on what isn't in our control. We just KNOW the difference.

How does mediation work? From a neuroscience perspective, research on meditators has shown drastic differences in brain structure—areas of the brain that support executive functioning, perspective taking, focus and working memory all increased, and areas that support anxiety, fear and stress decreased.

From an anecdotal perspective, let me share one of the first times I KNEW meditation was changing my brain: My husband and I were driving the kids to school one morning when he got a text from his sister. His dad and stepmom were going to be in town and they wanted to all get together for dinner on Friday night. We were supposed to have a much needed date night, but he rarely sees his dad so it was definitely something that he needed and wanted to do . . . but really, all things aside, I know he would've much rather had our date night. So he tells me the news, and I felt a knot rising up in me and I felt myself getting really angry at my husband. I noticed this and almost as if in slow motion, I looked at it with curiosity. I remember thinking, "huh, that is interesting, this is really triggering me. Why am I getting so worked up over this?" and I had all of this time and space to examine my feelings and look at it from a bunch of perspectives and I realized that my husband wasn't cancelling our dinner because he wanted to, and I was having an emotional reaction because of my own insecurities at the moment . . . but it had nothing to do with him . . . so I diffused my anger and treated him with kindness over having to cancel the dinner. In the past, I would've Just. Gotten. Mad. and behaved in a not so nice way presumably for awhile . . . I am sorry to admit. Possibly even days, without even being aware of why I was so worked up, and with my husband being baffled as well as to what happened to his sweet wife. I remember thinking after what felt like a minute or two (but really was just a few split seconds) how weird and superhuman it had felt, like I stopped time and had all of this insight and space that I never had before . . . and I knew it was from my meditation practice.

Tuning in and Letting Go

Another way I have been successful in improving my understanding of and practice of Surrender that goes hand in hand with mindfulness is to be very tuned into how my spirits feel. I keep my attention on how high or low I am feeling at any given moment, and I notice if I feel my spirits drop at all. Anytime that I feel a drop, I know something has gotten triggered in me that isn't healthy and that I need to Surrender to heal it. Whenever something is triggered, it is an opportunity in that moment to heal it by *letting it go*, whether I know what it is or not. Another way of feeling the trigger is when we get a knot rising up in us, from our throat, chest, gut or lower.

Being late was how I started figuring this out. I had just read Michael Singer's fabulous book, *Untethered Soul*, and he describes this "bubbling up" process when we get triggered. I had never heard of anything like it before and as I read his book I had absolutely no clue what he was talking about. I did already have an established meditation practice, so I was used to going "inside" and hanging out in that space of my inner energy, but his whole explanation about triggers bubbling up didn't make any sense at the time. But shortly after reading it, I was waiting for the subway, heading up to school to pick up my kids. And as was usually the case, I was cutting it close on time, and the subway was taking awhile to come. I felt this knot rising up and immediately my mind started going into overdrive to solve how I would NOT be late. I noticed all of this and told my mind to zip it (thanks to my meditation practice I have this awareness and power to quiet my mind). I tried to do what Michael Singer had described, getting under the bubble and letting it go up and out the top of my head without letting my mind try and push it back down. My mind pushing it back down is the denial of allowing what I fear to possibly happen—to try and explain it another way, as soon as we start to get triggered with pain, our mind tries to ensure that what we fear *will not happen*, as opposed to saying something like, "ok, I may be late, and even if that ends up happening, I will be ok".

It is a similar affirmation that I have shared with people, regardless of the situation—even if this worst case situation were to come to pass (and, be on point with what really is the probability of this worst case scenario, versus more likely unpleasant scenarios), I'm going to be ok.

Step one is taking *full responsibility* at all times for how I am feeling. No matter the situation, I deeply believe that no one has the power to "make me feel" bad (triggered) without me giving them that power. So if anything ever "makes me feel bad", I ask myself, why am I allowing that to bother me? That shifts the responsibility onto me, *and* gives me the power to heal and get stronger.

Step two is whenever I get triggered, I get out of my mind asap—the only exception is if there possibly is an external physical threat. If there is a possibility of a true physical threat, I want to use both my mind and intuition in conjunction—more on that when we talk about Fear. But assuming there isn't a physical threat, I want to get out of my mind and into my heart and make sure that I am keeping it open. Then, I let the pain rise up instead of pushing it back down.

There is this inner movement that, once you start to pay attention, you will feel, and it is almost like you need to hold space to allow the pain to rise up. Your heart will want to close and push the pain back down instead of letting it rise up, because you have to feel it when it rises up . . . and depending on what just got triggered, it may be really, really painful, and it may feel impossible to face it. Sometimes we need to ask for help and support from people that we love to help us hold space for the pain, and sometimes the pain is too much even then, and we may need to offload some of it on others, or distract ourselves, in order to let a little up and out at a time, instead of all at once. This may all sound nutty if you have never paid attention to inner pain, but I promise if you start pay attention and play around with this, hopefully starting on small things like being late, it will start to make some sense.

Our triggers, if allowed to throw us into Fight or Flight, hinder our ability to be compassionate and put us into a place of fear. The more we can root them out and replace them with faith in ourselves and faith in whatever larger forces are at work in this universe of ours, the stronger we will be. Surrender is that practice. This goes hand in hand with practicing forgiveness, which requires the same Surrender of our wound—we have to Surrender to reclaim our power and heal.

"Serenity Box"

Another powerful practice for Surrender is a "Serenity Box". In case you aren't familiar with the Serenity Prayer, it is: Grant me the Courage to change the things I can change, the Serenity to accept the things that I cannot and the Wisdom to the know the difference.

My business partner at Beacon, the brilliant Molly Carmel, gave me a box when I first started working with her and she explained that I was to write everything that I was worried about but ultimately was out of my hands on pieces of paper and put the pieces of paper in the box. Once you put them in the box, you had to let them go and know that they were in the Universe's hands. Trust in the Universe to be working them out however they needed to be worked out, and Surrender to what was going to happen.

The physical practice of writing whatever you are worried about and then folding up the paper and putting it in the box gives a tangible ritual to an abstract concept, and it helps you figure out the practice of Surrender. It starts to create a pathway where perhaps there hasn't been one before, and eventually you may find just the idea of the box is enough to help you practice Surrender.

Another funny story from a few years ago that showed me how powerful of a practice this was: one day, as usual, I was going to pick the kids up from school and we had about 5 minutes to get from school to an appointment that was 15 minutes away. The kids would need a snack, so I hit the little cafe that was right next to the school, inside the YMCA. The cafe doesn't have an outside entrance, so you have to go into the Y to get to it, and when I went in the lights were out and there was a sign on the door that said, "Closed for Renovations". Now first, before you think that I was over reacting, let me tell you that this is the only place to get a snack on the block, and life being as hectic as it is, that cafe being closed was devastating. So, when I saw that sign, my spirit immediately sunk to the floor. I walked to the main desk at the Y entrance and put my arms and head down on the desk in defeat. "How can they be closed? How long will it be?" I moaned. (The girls there know me so they felt my pain!) They agreed that it was a bummer and they hadn't been told either and didn't know how long it would be. As I laid there on the desk, the thought hit me and I blurted out as I perked up my head, "I can put it in my God Box!" (feel free to call it a Serenity Box or God Box, doesn't matter! But at the time I called mine a God Box) The girl laughed and said, "I don't know what that is but it sounds great!" And my spirits immediately lifted as I realized in one fell swoop what and where I needed to Surrender and even more importantly, I was able to Surrender! (It was closed for four days and somehow I survived.)

Overcoming the Need to Know WHY

Another example of how we get stuck and need to practice Surrender is around our need to know WHY things happen. This is again, an evolutionarily important instinct and desire—after all, when something painful happens, our brain wants to know the cause so we can avoid it in the future. This is obviously hugely helpful when trying to stay alive. Did you ever notice how much less apt we are to ask WHY when something good happens? Unless we are suspicious of there possibly being something nefarious behind it! Our brain doesn't have the same wired survival instinct to get to the bottom of good things!

The problem is that, when we can't see the *why*, our brain won't give up trying to find the *why* . . . and it gets stuck. It won't accept the pain because it can't make sense of it in the way that it is programed to, so it will just keep going around in circles. Even if you aren't aware of this consciously, it continues subconsciously. It can't integrate the experience and file it neatly away, so it remains an "open case". The problem with this is that everytime something happens that somehow resembles anything associated with the "open case" our brain jumps up, metaphorically, and yells EUREKA!—we get triggered with a jolt of fear, even though there isn't really a threat. We talked about this a lot when we discussed Courage, because we need to learn how to handle these triggers.

But wait, is Surrender the key to avoiding MORE triggers? Yes. Yes it. And the key lies in overcoming our need to know WHY things happen. We need to get over that. Yes, we need to learn from things that go wrong, absolutely—we need to get as close to our pain and fear and learn EVERYTHING that we can from it. But at some point, we need to Surrender that we can't ever know all of the WHYs. There is something bigger going on here that our brain can't ever make rational sense of. So, learn as much as you can, and then Surrender to the fact that we can't know everything. And it is what it is.

In college "It is what it is" became one of my favorite mantras. I don't remember how I started saying it, but it gave me so much solace in the face of irrational suffering. Nothing about what I was going through made any sense, and the little bit of help I got in Surrendering came from that mantra. I highly recommend practicing that when things don't make sense and there is pain—if you say, "It is what it is", while breathing up and out, it is really a helpful practice.

I also recommend trying out a few different perspectives on this, depending on how you feel about having faith in something bigger than yourself. If you like to say Universe or God or Life Force or the bigger picture, you can insert any of those concepts into the mix. A friend once shared something she overheard that really resonated with me: God is a bird that flies far overhead and can see things that we cannot see. We can't always know why things happen, and we need to figure out how to accept that and override our brain's impulse to get stuck...leaving the triggered to be hit later on like land mines. One of the hardest examples of Surrender, and oh-so important to work on.

As I've often recommended in this book, start practicing when it is easy! When the unexpected things aren't so painful. Notice when something goes "wrong" in a little way, and your mind's desire to fight it and want to know *why*. Notice how you can Surrender the need to know *why* with a laugh, because it is no big deal. And notice how ridiculous it would be to always want to know *why*—like if you were at a restaurant and ordered the salmon, but they came back and said, "I'm so sorry but we are actually out of the salmon"—you wouldn't (hopefully) bang your head down on the table and say "WHY?!? OH WHY?! How could you be out of the salmon?!?" No, because it isn't that big of a deal. So notice that and give yourself a positive wink when you are able to Surrender on the little things, so you will be more skilled when you need to Surrender on the big things.

At the end of the day, becoming more skillful at practicing Surrender is what allows our life to flow, allows grace to be present and allows US to be present. Without Surrender we will be stuck in our heads, either hanging onto the past or trying to control the future, and we will miss living and loving our life.

SURRENDER BONUS: Synergy and Clarity

When we are not in a state of Surrender, we are interfering with how things are unfolding, not from a place of love, but from a place fear. When we Surrender, we stop interfering with how life is naturally unfolding and we are able to respond with positive contributions. When you have two or more people who are able to respond to life as it is unfolding with positive contributions, you get synergy. Synergy is defined as the interaction or cooperation to produce a combined effect greater than the sum of their separate effects. 1+1=3 (or more!) This is able to happen when we are open to trusting those who we come into contact with, and trust the overall situation. We are then able to openly collaborate and experience the power of synergy. We are able to literally ride the wave of creativity to heights we never could have on our own, individual power. Synergy takes our own power and multiplies it exponentially. It takes our greatest personal achievements to entirely new heights.

We all hopefully have had the experience when we meet someone and they seem to bring out the best of us, and we bring out the best in them. We can feel that they believe in us and only want good things for us, and we feel the same way about them. It is those feelings that are clues that you are Surrendering and feeling faith in both yourself and the other person and can experience synergy together. It is a beautiful thing.

The other unexpected bonus of Surrender is Clarity. When we stop interfering with the flow of life, is it almost like we stop stirring up muddy water, or we stop the ripples on the water . . . and things finally become clear. We can just SEE what we need to do and it is clear what sparks Joy. This clarity is our greatest power, because we no longer need to waste any energy on anything other than our noble work. However we are meant to be of service, our love, our laughter, our creativity, our inspiration, our work will be clear. More on this when we talk about intuition.

Chapter 5

OPENNESS/CURIOSITY

You can never REALLY know everything about a situation.

— *Pamela Palladino Gold*

Truly, I am serious and this is *critical*. (To those of you who counter, ok, but I know ENOUGH—that is your Ego talking. Tell it to zip it.)

Our mind wants us to feel like we know that we are right, because that is how we feel safe, and admitting that we don't really know . . . feels vulnerable as hell! And our mind really, *really* hates that, so it creates this illusion of knowing as a form of self protection. There are many downfalls to this illusion—for one, it stops our evolution. We can't learn anything new if we think we already know. Plus, if we are incorrect in what we think, there will be negative consequences (aka learning opportunities) whether we want them or now, as we get hit over the proverbial head with whatever we were wrong about. The truth always comes out eventually.

It takes mindfulness to start to break this illusion, because we have been participating in this for so long that for many of us, there is zero awareness that what we think we know is actually a judgment as opposed to a fact. And then, there are layers of things that we think we know, that we rely on to think that we know other things, and so on and so on. (Read that a few times.) It is a giant illusion. And it's scary as hell to start to dismantle it . . . so it's time to practice bravery my friends. Buckle up. You cannot be Open and Curious without Courage.

And, you have to get comfortable with being wrong. I know, our Ego *hates* to be wrong—it immediately feels "not good enough" and you get that knot in your stomach . . . but that is SO WRONG (pun intended)! Whenever we find that we are wrong, we have grown! If you haven't seen Kathryn Schultz's brilliant TED Talk "On Being Wrong", it is a must watch. Being wrong is exciting and fabulous, just keep telling yourself that. We need to erase our fear of being wrong, or it will be really hard to practice Openness.

Judgement and Closed Mindedness

The opposite of Openness is Judgment or Closed Mindedness. If we judge something as Right or Wrong, Good or Bad, or think in any way that we KNOW EVERYTHING that there is to know about a situation, or enough to judge it or label it, we are not practicing Openness.

If we judge something or someone as "Bad" we close our hearts to them and close our minds to the idea that there might be more to the situation than we can see or know. It is much easier to deal with a situation by judging it—you can just label it and move on. But of course, labels only tell a partial story and are often quite misleading. There is always more to the story, and usually the deeper you go, the more important the information is.

We know this if we are parents. Our kids are generally well behaved kids (hopefully) . . . but if they are tired or hungry or sick or scared or in pain, watch out. I remember one day we took the kids to the Discovery Museum in Times Square and Jesse was about 4 at the time. As we finished the exhibit there was a cupcake kiosk with an array of cupcakes to choose from. I was agreeable, so the kids placed their orders. Jesse wanted Chocolate. Cupcakes were handed over in smooth fashion in a box and we went and sat down to eat the cupcakes. Well, upon opening the box it was discovered that the Chocolate cupcake had a bit of whipped cream squiggles on it.

Cue meltdown. Me, sighing as I realized just how overtired Jesse was, feeling the glares of the people around us...I start trying to lick off the whipped cream squigglies as Jesse escalates to a full on "I DON'T WANT THAT CUPCAKE, I WANT CHOCOLATE" and proceeds to throw the cupcake box across the room. It was a stellar moment. Literally, anyone would've looked at that display and come to the very reasonable conclusion that my son was a complete brat and I was a horrible, over indulgent and poorly skilled parent. But, I knew there was more to the story. He was freaking exhausted. It doesn't excuse the behavior, but at 4, it pretty much comes with the territory if you have a "spirited" child (aka sensitive and reactive) . . .

As parents, we know our children so well, and we still miss cues and make judgments that are wrong. There was a time that Talia just started behaving SO BADLY out of nowhere, so disrespectful and impatient and out of character for her . . . I honestly thought she was testing me or something and I was pretty harsh with her . . . and then she spiked a 103 fever. Parenting fail.

I use parenting as an example because not only can we relate to judging our kids, but we all have felt judged as parents . . . and not only does it feel like crap, but it is *wrong*. We are all doing our best and these other people *do not know our kids like we do*. They cannot possibly judge if what we are doing is best or not. It is ridiculous, and we know it. Yet, if we aren't mindful, we go about our day consistently doing it to others, perhaps on a smaller scale.

Driving is another great example. If you drive, you've experienced someone cutting you off, or getting right on your tail super fast when there was no way for you to get over and they swerve in the other lane and almost take everyone out as they fly past you. Of course, the explanation could be that this person is just a horrible driver and a jerk, but there is absolutely no way to know what is going on in that car. For all we know, that person could be trying to get to the hospital to see their child who was in a horrible accident. Judging the situation as negative doesn't do any good what so ever, it simply pisses us off and makes it more likely that we make a poor choice while driving. If we find an alternative perspective as opposed to judging, it will make us more powerful and happy.

Staying Open and Curious keeps our power in our control, as opposed to what our mind thinks. And, it keeps this power *flowing* as opposed to getting stuck.

So Pam, how do you propose we go through life if we aren't supposed to judge? Just put our heads in the sand? Clearly, no. Here is where I like to use the word ASSESS. Which some people read quickly as asses. But it isn't Asses. It is Assess.

Asses Judge. Don't be an Ass, Assess

Assess the hell out of everything, and don't stop. Keep getting more info. This is Openness. This is Curiosity. We could also use the word investigate. But that doesn't read like Asses. ;)

Investigator Extraordinaire

Being an investigator feels Open and Powerful. You stay curious and engaged in everything in your life. This allows your Spiritual Strength to build and flow. So channel your inner Sherlock Holmes (or Magnum PI or Angela Lansbury, you pick) and get to work:

- Look for things that are unexpected or unusual. Train yourself to notice those surprises and enjoy them!

- Look for meaning in each moment. That may be kindness, learning, laughter, creativity, inspiration...
- Look for clues as to what you might not know that you don't know.
- Ask yourself and others open questions.
- Talk less and practice deep listening.
- Catch yourself making assumptions and kindly and gently remind yourself to go back into deeper investigation.
- Use the mantra: More Shall Be Revealed.

Obviously this is far out of most of our comfort zones and involves a lot of the Surrender and Courage skills we already hit on. Just know that this Openness and Curiosity facilitates your strength and evolution! Especially when you are out of your comfort zone.

Inner Siren vs. Out of Your Comfort Zone

We talked a bit earlier about trusting our intuition and listening to our inner siren. If we get a gut feeling that something is off, we need to investigate it. At the same time, trying something new, taking risks, being out of our comfort zone is SUPPOSED to feel uncomfortable. So in those moments when you are feeling uncomfortable, how do you know if it is your inner siren telling you something is wrong or if it is just that you are out of your comfort zone making some magic happen?? You need to investigate! Is there really a potential threat in the situation or is it just that your ego is feeling vulnerable to the high probably that you are going to make a fool out of yourself as you fall 180 times trying to learn to windsurf? Our mind will come up with all kinds of crazy excuses as to why we shouldn't do something that is vulnerable to our ego.

Seriously, I remember a few years ago when I decided I wanted to learn to windsurf and it was on the beach in front of everyone out there enjoying their vacation, and I literally had never tried to Wind Surf before, so I needed to embrace that I was going to make a fool of myself. I was nervous, but I could look at the situation and see that there wasn't any real threat in what I was about to do, I was just going to grow from it! So I shut that part of my mind off and went out there and kept getting back on the board (the instructor was right there with me the whole time, so literally I had nothing to worry about). It was an awesome day . . . but if I had a closed mind I never would've done it.

We need to be super mindful about the stories our mind will make up to try and get us out of brave, investigator mode—we have to be vigilant to not let this happen if we want to build our Spiritual Strength.

What do we really know?

I often ask myself, OK, what do I really know? How do I know what I think is true to be really true? For real, no bullshit? Because I know if I assume something to be true that isn't true, I'm going to be in for a fall, and I'd rather not learn that lesson the hard way. By asking questions before hand, I can hopefully identify fact from fiction and make better moves, and get better results. Why wouldn't we all want that? In the long term we want to live great lives, leave a legacy of great work, regardless if it is big or small, we want it to be great! And if we make moves based on incorrect assumptions, things aren't going to turn out great until we correct course.

Keep asking questions, staying open at all times and learning something from everyone you meet—this will serve you and your Spiritual Strength in leaps and bounds.

Joy vs. Pleasure

Another important area of Openness and Curiosity is figuring out the difference between joy and pleasure. Joy comes from the inside out and leaves us higher than we were before. We derive joy from being in alignment with our true selves and sharing positivity with those around us. Meaningful relationships, generosity, compassion, wisdom, courage, creativity, laughter, being in nature, engaging in activities that expand our awareness and make us feel loved, learning and alive give us joy.

Pleasure, on the other hand, comes from the outside in, lasts for only a short while and leaves us lower than we were before. Indulging in the 5 senses, having external validation of how awesome you are, experiencing something thrilling but perhaps out of alignment with what is in your best interests or out of alignment with what you *really* want for yourself, are a few examples of where we can find pleasure. Food, imbalanced relationships, drugs and alcohol, taking inflated risks/acting impulsively are all examples of things that can give us pleasure.

Our lower brain loves pleasure as much as joy and couldn't care less about the difference. Evolutionarily, this is obviously thanks to the two powerful human instincts of self-survival and reproduction – but it doesn't serve the deeper goals of our lives. Pleasure is often a short term reality, especially in our current society with so many engineered indulgences. 500 years ago, things were much simpler. If you came across any type of yummy food, eating it and as much of it as possible was pretty much definitely in your best interest. Nowadays, not so much.

Eating food that is actually good for you gives you a deep joy that you are honoring your body and health and supporting your long term goals. Eating something yummy will give you pleasure, and depending on how overboard you go on it, it is working against your health and long term goals, and often ends up having the effect of us groaning inwardly or aloud "Ugh, I wish I hadn't eaten that".

Only you can know, in any given moment, if something is a source of joy or a source of pleasure—no one can judge you, just like you can't judge anyone else. We want to figure out what brings us joy and follow that. Conversely, we want to be as mindful as possible when we are seeking pleasure or indulging in pleasure and steer away from that. On any given day, at any given moment, the exact same thing could be a source of joy or we could be using it as a source of pleasure.

We can enjoy something with our five senses, and a test as to whether it is joy or pleasure is asking, "how do we feel when it is taken away?". If we are attaching to it, and losing it leaves us feeling low, it is likely pleasure. Joy flows. A bit of ice cream or no ice cream, either way you are happy? Then it is joy. You are enjoying it from the inside out. If you are using ice cream for pleasure, and you might not get any, you are likely to be upset. Joy feels like a spark, pleasure feels like a seeking.

Being open and curious about the difference between joy and pleasure in your life is a powerful practice that can bring a huge shift to your life and Spiritual Strength. And at the end of the day, all of our practices of Openness and Curiosity represents our outward growth—branches that manifest as Love, Laughter, Learning, Creativity and Inspiration. As we practice Openness and Curiosity in all areas of our life, we will find more and more Love, Laughter, Learning, Creativity and Inspiration in our lives. And, more Spiritual Strength as we move towards unlocking unlimited power and happiness.

OPENNESS/CURIOSITY BONUS: Intuition

Practicing Openness and Curiosity helps us start to listen to our intuition. There is an inner knowing that we have available to us, if we get quiet and listen. Things that we literally could not possibly know, start to just come to us. Since you are already practicing Openness and Curiosity, just be open to it. Your intuition is quiet, where as your mind is loud, so you need to start to quiet your mind to be able to hear it . . . but start to play with it a bit and I bet you will start to notice a quiet voice that is different from how your mind usually chimes in. You can ask yourself questions and listen for that quiet voice. One I really recommend trying, when you are unsure of what to do: ask yourself, "What would love do?" It is open ended enough that your intuition will tell you what is right for you. Love will always guide your best decisions, as opposed to fear, which will always lead to suffering at some point. It is always the spirit behind the decisions, as opposed to the decision themselves, that determine the ultimate outcome.

Listening to our intuition will bring sometimes funny or unbelievable occurrences. In November, the day after the Trump victory, I was walking through Rockefeller Center, underground by all the shops. It was a pretty dark day in NYC and the heaviness was palpable. As I walked towards the subway, I saw a flower stand up ahead and felt the impulse to buy someone flowers. My mind immediately started to protest: Who are you going to buy flowers for? No one in NYC just wants to randomly be given flowers, because you have no where to put them. Bring them to Talia's teacher? That was still at least 45 minutes away and I was loaded down with my gym bag, computer, etc. My mind was full of worthy reasons why this made no sense. But still, the impulse felt very strong, so I walked over to the flower stand. I looked at the flowers, none of them really speaking to me, my mind still full of obstacles to my generous impulse. As I stood there in line, the person in front of me was handed her flowers, and I heard the exchange as she handed over her credit card: "I'm so sorry, we only take cash. How much cash do you have on you? Only $2? Well you can come back later and pay . . . you won't be back in the area? Just visiting a friend who just had surgery?" . . . you can imagine where I am going with this. I excitedly proclaimed that I would be glad to buy the flowers for her and her friend. When she protested I explained how I came over to buy someone flowers but I had no idea who I was buying flowers for, and now I knew! She agreed to accept, I paid and walked away feeling so happy I listened to my intuition.

Part Two

Beyond The Pillars

Chapter 6

AWARENESS, PERSPECTIVE & EPIPHANIES

Who looks outside dreams; who looks inside, awakes.

— *Carl Jung*

The real goal of all of this work is to keep "leveling up". As we figure out more of these truths and experience their power, everything shifts and there is no going back. It is like climbing a mountain and each time you get to a higher ledge you can see things you just simply couldn't before, and now you KNOW what is really there. With that knowledge comes the power to navigate whatever is in front of you with new seemingly superhuman grace and ease. Until it gets hard again and you have to level up again. And more of the illusion dissipates. It's a beautiful process.

The first step is awareness. Notice what you are paying attention to, instead of letting your attention flying around like it was out of your control. Practicing Mindfulness is like doing bicep curls for your brain. The more you practice, the more powerful your control will be.

Be aware of when your Ego is driving the ship and be wary of it's limited assessments (are you looking for external validation? Comparisons? Taking things personally? That's all Ego.)—feel what it is like to have your heart and your head out of alignment versus in alignment, and be very mindful when something feels off.

Once you have awareness you can have a wider perspective. A wider perspective is when you can start to look at the big picture of things, more than just what you are experiencing in that one moment or from just the one perspective your brain can initially see . . . and you can start to see your tiny part in it all. I mean really, really tiny. Joseph Campbell[13] says, it is both true that you are the hero in your own epic journey and simultaneously just one of a million plus warriors out on the battlefield in a huge epic battle. Both are true, and this perspective is powerful.

Keeping things in perspective is a wonderful practice in and of itself, helping us practice our 5 pillars of Gratitude, Compassion, Courage, Surrender and Openness/Curiosity, because by definition we can see beyond just our own experience in that one moment. It helps us remain Grateful in the face of challenges, helps us find Compassion for ourself and others in the face of less than ideal behavior or outcomes, find Courage knowing

---

[13]American mythologist, writer and lecturer, best known for his work in comparative mythology and comparative religion. His work covers many aspects of the human experience.

that we are stronger than we may feel at that moment, find faith enough to Surrender things out of our control and be Open to the things that we know we can't know yet. Keeping things in perspective is a synthesis of all of our practices, really.

Then, we have our epiphanies. Ultimately, it is our epiphanies that connect the dots in our wider perspective enabling us to shift to a higher level of understanding—we have whatever perspective we currently have and then BOOM—holy cow, we can now see a pattern, a deeper truth, that we couldn't see a minute ago. And, everything changes.

I've always been a bit obsessed with epiphanies because I knew that they were huge when it came to being strong and living my best life. I can remember a lot of epiphanies I've had over the years—epiphanies tend to be pretty memorable because after you have one, everything changes . . . and sometimes that is not a good feeling at first.

There was one I will never forget, I was sitting in the house that I grew up in, in the study area on the phone, trying to have a semi-private phone call with my long distance "boyfriend". I was 12, he was 15. Things weren't going well, we were having a hard time connecting, I was doing my best but I was a lot younger . . . oh so unskilled and oh so unaware. So he was frustrated with me, and I can still hear him saying, "You know, not everyone thinks the way you do, Pam." And actually, up until that moment, no, I hadn't really figured that out yet. I had been operating under this noble but admittedly rather unsophisticated "treat people the way you want to be treated" precept . . . but that got shot to hell as the realization that this wasn't *enough* because just because I would like to be treated a certain way, it doesn't mean that someone else wants to be treated that way. I remember being crushed and lost in that moment, as often epiphanies initially feel—as the old way of seeing things gets shattered, we are often left clueless in those initial moments as to how the heck to relate to our new world now that we no longer see it as we just did. And our mind doesn't like that in the least.

So often, the big epiphanies are incredibly destabilizing . . . but there are lots of little epiphanies that can feel less vulnerable and more like liberating wins, thank goodness. They can be small a-ha moments when something that was stuck not-quite-right falls into place and life gets that much lighter, clearer or easier. But very often even little epiphanies or realizations of knowing, are immediately followed with what is a reflexive Fight or Flight response in our body and in our mind. This is our fear keeping us locked in the prior illusion. To change means to move out of our comfort zone, out of what the mind can make sense of and try and control. The bigger the epiphany, the bigger the fear that can come with it. This is because of everything we have talked about at length in this book: our mind is wired for survival in this world first. It has to be because without survival we wouldn't be in the position to even be having this conversation! Our brain (which creates an emotional response that we feel in our entire body) is trying to keep us safe, and instinctively chooses safety over higher wisdom. The mind would rather judge and feel safe and stay in a more limited awareness of only the things that it can see and make sense of, than accept the deeper realizations that are not linear and it can't make rational sense of. Again, the Little Prince quote, "It is only with the heart that one can see rightly." The amount of resistance in the mind is what keeps us from "leveling up".

What is it specifically that helps us connect the dots and suddenly have an epiphany? Perspective and awareness play a big part, as does everything else we've covered so far: Gratitude, Humility, Compassion, Courage, Surrender, Openness and Curiosity. Ultimately it is out of our greatest pain that we have our biggest epiphanies. And little pain points are what lead to all of our a-ha moments, whether we are aware of it or not. If it weren't for our pain points, we wouldn't be looking for answers. We wouldn't be seeking.

I have a deeper hypothesis of why this is, but that is a whole other book. What is important now is to use these tools KNOWING that they WORK. Don't take my word for it! Practice and see how you feel and how your life changes.

5 Pillars at Work

The more we continually expand our awareness and perspective in our lives, the more we can start to figure out patterns that can help us suddenly have an epiphany. Practicing Gratitude and Humility connects us to a center "Ground" of who we really are and being open to receive our blessings. Practicing Courage and Surrender keeps us "Centered", not wasting energy on things that are out of our control, but focusing our energy on the things that benefit from our energy. Courage and Surrender help us face our fears and allow the pain and move through the pain instead of pushing it down—and it is through the experience of our pain that we grow up and out of it. Practicing Openness and Curiosity keeps us, obviously, "Open" so life can continue to flow through us and we keep evolving with our expanded awareness and perspectives, and not get stuck in our pain. Any one of these areas being blocked will hold us back. And we will feel lost and/or trapped and/or stuck . . . and growth will either be slow or not at all.

I distinctly remember the darkest period of my life when I was in college and I felt very lost and trapped. It was a really rough combination of, at the root of it, not really knowing who I was and at the same time being in a lot of pain and not seeing any way of making things better. In deep pain, feeling completely lost and hopeless.

As I've mentioned, it had become apparent very early on in my freshman year at college that my boyfriend, Josh, had a drug problem. I remember getting a calendar and deciding that for every day that I knew he used, I would circle the day in red . . . so I could look back and actually assess the situation and trust in what I thought I knew (he of course was saying that I was crazy, and I felt crazy, that's for sure). Needless to say, the calendar was all red, and I knew I wasn't crazy.

The thing about being in the thick of it, being in the weeds or lost like that, is that you can't see the answer to your problem. You can't see in that moment that 20 years from now you will look back and be so grateful for all of the learning opportunities that pain presented. You don't see that you will be ok even if the person that you love isn't. You are stuck seeing it from your perspective, and your pain, which doesn't allow you to see the big picture yet.

In that moment, you are in *so much pain* and you *need it to stop* and you don't know how to make it stop.

So, I remember weeks when I rarely got out of bed during the day and I'd go out at night to get drunk and do whatever brought me joy or pleasure (I always liked to have fun, truly loved experiencing life, which is a good thing because it was one of the things that always kept me going—I was brave and reckless as hell—and definitely had no clue about the difference between joy and pleasure)—behaviors that obviously weren't going to solve my problems. I am sure I seemed lazy and irresponsible. I was just in the weeds trying to figure out how to get through each day.

Looking back now, I can see how I lacked Gratitude, lacked Self-Compassion and lacked Surrender. I had a ton of outward Compassion, Courage and Openness/ Curiosity and that is what enabled me to continue to grow through that period, albeit in a very messy (very very messy) way. If I had Gratitude and Self-Compassion, it would've grounded me in a way that would've enabled me to grow through that period perhaps in a less messy way. Surrender I think is the most sophisticated of all of these practices, and perhaps the most transformative, because if I imagine myself figuring out Surrender at a younger age, that is the skill that really allows the flow of life to *flow*. But I was doing my best at the time from my level of awareness.

Buddhism Principles

Another way of explaining this *flow* is to talk about the Buddhist principles of Non-Attachment, Non-Resistance and Non-Judgment. If we are Surrendering, we are not interfering with what IS. That isn't to say that we don't work really hard each moment of our lives to be of service in all ways as much possible—when we Surrender and stop feeling the need to interfere with life we actually start to find that we have infinitely more inspiration and creativity and purpose and passion to work harder than ever, with enthusiasm and joy in everything that we do! We simply are allowing the flow of life around us to unfold without the need to manipulate it to fit some "need" of ours. We do not attach or cling to anything in our lives, we allow anything we love to flow. We do not resist anything in our lives, so any pain or death that would typically be an aversion we accept and lean in to see what it is meant to teach us. We do not judge anything as good or bad or right or wrong, because it all is as it is, and it is all part of one.

I remember reading passages like this in the philosophy books I studied starting at a young age and being stumped as to what the heck it really meant and how it could be. My boyfriend (post-breaking up with Josh) at Yale was a philosophy major and wrote his senior thesis on Martin Buber's *I and Thou*, and we tried so hard to come up with what he was really talking about in that book. But it wasn't until my consciousness evolved to the point that it is now that I could understand—the words themselves don't make sense until your awareness is at the point of being able to connect with the concepts. And it takes practice for most of us to get our consciousness to evolve, to have the epiphanies, to keep leveling up so that our "best" can get better and better. It is this deepest, ultimate sense of connection that Buber is talking about, but the words themselves will forever be inadequate alone to convey this meaning...until we experience it for ourselves.

Meditation and Expanding Awareness

Establishing a regular meditation practice with concentrated effort in the beginning is a powerful key to unlocking a lot of this. The power of our attention is what allows us to have the basic awareness of whether we are even practicing the 5 pillars at any given moment.

The first stage of meditation is continued focus on a single focal point. This is really hard at first but like everything else, practice makes progress. There are so many options for beginning a meditation practice, but you can start simply at home listening to online tracks. One of my teachers, Alan Finger, has meditations on Spotify.

The second stage of meditation is effortless continued focus. This is important to know, because once you get proficient at the first stage, being able to keep your attention on one focal point, you can remember that it being *effortless* is what comes next and what you want to be moving toward. The third stage is when you start to experience oneness. There is no set amount of time as to how long it takes to experience it, but the practice brings so many transformative benefits, it is worth the patience and effort. There are many different types of meditation and techniques and you want to find something that works for you. Seek out a teacher that feels like a good fit. Generally, it is best to stick with one technique with the goal of increasing how deep you go and for how long. The more time you spend in deep meditation, the quicker you can expand your awareness.

Besides mediation, which is the most effective way that I have experienced, there are other simple ways of expanding our awareness: being in nature, traveling, reading, meeting new people, being Open and Curious to anything that is out of your comfort zone. All of this is expanding your awareness. So do all that as much as possible.

You are not your body

A major epiphany is that you are not your body. Your body is like a rental car that you were gifted for this experience of your human life on this planet. Your body is made up of roughly 3 trillion cells, many of which aren't human but rather bacterial. I don't know how we could think that the raging miracle metropolis that is cooperating to allow us to be here is really *us*, but since our brain can't really make sense of anything else, most of us get stuck identifying with our body. But stop to think about it, and feel it—feel the life that is pulsing through your body. Feel the cells and systems cooperating. It is a miracle, but it isn't really *you*. Once you realize that, as an example, everything changes. For one thing, you will feel deeply called to take better care of your body and be more grateful and compassionate with it. Once you realize this, it's just like if I said to you, "OK, you are going to get shot out into space in this spacecraft. Once the spacecraft breaks down, your journey will be over and you will no longer be able to continue on." You'd do everything that you can to take as good care of that spacecraft, right? You'd love and appreciate how awesome your spacecraft was to allow you to go on this amazing space voyage. And, you wouldn't judge each other by their spacecraft, since we all seemingly randomly ended up with different spacecrafts . . . it obviously wouldn't be our spacecraft that defines us, because we are so much more than that on the inside. But until we have that epiphany, we are all operating on another set of rules for how to best navigate being alive and human. How to make sense of it all. And we will be there until we aren't.

The biggest takeaway from all of this on awareness, perspective and epiphanies is that we are all doing the best that we can from wherever we are . . . from our level of awareness, whatever that is. If we want to better our lives, we need to work to expand our awareness and keep "leveling up" - this is the path to unlock unlimited power and happiness.

Overview of "Leveling Up"

Think of Russian nesting dolls: you have the smallest doll in the center, surrounded by a bigger doll, that is surrounded by a bigger doll, etc. Imagine that you are the littlest doll, and that is all you know. All of a sudden, the larger version of yourself comes along and BOOM, everything fits perfectly, it all matches up and now you are that bigger doll . . . again, it is all you know and all you can see and all that you think there is. But then, a larger doll shows up, again everything matching perfectly, and BOOM, now you are that bigger doll. Hopefully you see where I am going with this. It is a lot like the levels of awareness that we have, as I like to explain it.

Levels of awareness:

1. Victim: You see your life as happening to you and out of your control.
2. Hero: You realize that you have the power to be your own hero with your actions and tap into Courage.
3. Power of Thought: You realize that what you THINK actually changes your life, not just what you DO.
4. Of Service: You realize that we are all connected and nothing is really about you—you shift to wanting to be of service, instead of focusing first on your own gain.

5. Oneness: You realize that it isn't just that we are all connected in some way, but we are actually all ONE. Time and space is an illusion and your intuition is more powerful than anything your brain is capable of.

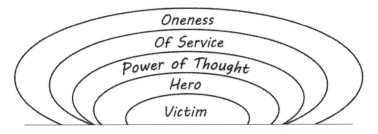

For the purposes of this book and unlocking unlimited power and happiness, if the 5 pillars are our foundational tools for building Spiritual Strength, this is our map for reaching our highest potential. The vast majority of humanity is oscillating between victim mode and hero mode. The fact that you are even reading this book means that you are in hero mode (or beyond) a lot of the time. People who are stuck in victim mode most of the time will not take the initiative to read a book like this. Victims are reacting to life as opposed to being proactive to make their life better. They are stuck closed to trying something that might help, convinced that it won't. The first thing that has to happen with someone stuck in victim mode is that there needs to be an opening, and each person is unique as to the best way to accomplish that.

The tricky thing about our levels of awareness (or levels of consciousness) is that we bounce around. Most of us have times when we are in the hero mode (or beyond) but then we get triggered and end up back down in victim mode often without realizing it. When we are in victim mode, we are not practicing the 5 pillars and we are in our lower states, below Courage. It is really important that we learn how to navigate those states when we find ourselves triggered and getting stuck there.

Chapter 7

OUR LOWEST STATES

"Greatness is the courage to overcome obstacles."

—David R. Hawkins, Letting Go:
The Pathway of Surrender

In David Hawkin's brilliant book, **Letting Go**, he maps out our states of consciousness, or another way of putting it, our levels of spirit, from lowest to highest vibrational frequency. I was so excited when I was introduced to his book, because since I was a little kid I was always obsessed with trying to show spatially how I was feeling. I always felt that there was an up and down sensation associated with feelings and I knew that this was important to figuring out how to be the best me I could be. Shame, Guilt, Apathy, Grief and Fear are the lowest, respectively, and it is important to understand them so you can know them when you feel them and have a sense of how to rise up out of them. Courage is the first level that is positive, meaning that we have the capability to add positivity to our outside world, and anything below that has a negative impact on our world. Knowing how you are feeling is the first step, and getting clarity on all of this is key to being able to be strong spiritually.

Brené Brown defined Shame as feeling unworthy of love or unworthy of connection to something bigger than yourself. I love this definition because I think it clarifies what is really going on with us when we are feeling Shame. We think that we are *so awful* that we are unworthy of love. I feel like we need to pause there for a minute, because all of us carry around Shame, whether we are aware of it or not, and I want you to take a moment to try and connect to Shame within you. Can you think of something that you are ashamed of, or something that happened once that you are ashamed of? Can you feel what that feels like in your body? For me, I feel it in the pit of my stomach, and that is super important because anytime you feel it, it is an opportunity to let it come up and go.

So now, if you feel up to it, take a pause and remember in great detail as much as you can about what it is that you are ashamed of and feel that pain come up in you—let yourself really feel that pain—know that you are ok and loved and supported as you feel it and accept the pain as you remind yourself that you are ok. Don't let your mind get involved in this narrative, just ask yourself, what did you learn from this? And tell yourself that it is ok to forgive yourself and anyone else involved, you learned from it and can let it go. And try and let the feeling just go up and out of you as you forgive and let light and love in to take its place inside of you. There is *nothing* that can ever happen to you and/or *no mistake* that you can ever make that makes you unworthy of love. *You are not your mistakes.* It is time to take full responsibility and learn from whatever the painful event was, because it was an opportunity for growth, no matter how painful and messy, and it is time to rise up from it.

The next level up from Shame is Guilt. Guilt isn't as low as Shame, but it is still pretty low. Guilt is having the weight of believing that in some way, you weren't/ aren't good enough. Again, we all have Guilt that we are carrying around. This weighs us down, literally and figuratively. The more spiritual weight we are carrying around, the harder it is to keep our spirits up. And to be clear, none of these states are *bad* - they just are and we need to love whatever IS . . . and that love is how we learn and heal and get spiritually strong. So, same thing we did with Shame—ask yourself quietly, what do you feel Guilty about? Listen for a quiet answer. That quiet answer is your deeper knowing. Take the time to let it come up, face the situation, and just like we did with Shame, ask what did I/can I learn from this situation— it happened to *teach* you something, and fully accepting the pain of it is necessary to fully integrate the growth. Let it all come up and, keeping your mind from getting involved in blaming, denying, offloading, let it go up and out. Visualize light and loven shining it to replace it. And remember, we are always doing our best from whatever our level of what we can see! Guilt is there to teach us, not to weigh us down.

Apathy, not caring, is the next level up from Guilt. We all know that low feeling of just not caring in the least, feeling cold and cut off. In some ways it feels good because it is an improvement from feeling Shame or Guilt, but it is still soooooo low. You are not feeling love or connection in the least. You can ask yourself now, is there something that I just don't care about? Apathy is always pain of some kind that we are burying, and just like with Shame and Guilt, we need to allow it to rise up, to face the pain, so we can fully experience it and fully grow from it, letting the light and love of forgiveness in to replace it. I should add that it isn't always necessary to *know* what exactly the issue is that is causing us pain. We can let it go without having any clue what it is that is going on with us, and it is equally healing.

One of my yoga teachers at ISHTA had this brilliant analogy of imagining that you forgot a bag of groceries, produce of all things!, in the trunk of your car for three months. Three months later you discover this bag of absolute horror—it is just gross, gushy, rotting mush. *You just get that bag out of your car ASAP!* Do not try to figure out if it had been cucumbers and tomatoes and onions . . . or perhaps it was tomatoes and mangoes and peppers . . . For goodness sake it doesn't matter! *Just get rid of it!*

Same goes for any of these lower states of baggage that you are carrying it around. You don't even need to know what the heck the pain is associated with. Just by practicing this technique of release whenever you feel it, you will be getting rid of it, at least a little bit at a time, and it won't pop up as much next time. You can release everything around an entire huge issue in your life without even realizing that you did. This can happen in ways that don't make rational sense. You may be getting a massage or a chiropractic adjustment and just start crying for no apparent reason. Maybe you are watching a telephone commercial and all of sudden are overwhelmed with emotion. As long as you let it up and out as opposed to pushing it back down/ denying it, you are releasing some sort of lower state baggage.

I experienced this a few years ago after doing my 5 week intensive yoga teaching program. There was a lot of stuff that came up during that program but at no point was I aware of even thinking about the pain of losing Josh to his drug addiction. Prior to the yoga program, we only spoke every now and then, maybe once every couple of years, but every time that we talked I had knots in my stomach. I still carried so much guilt over ending the relationship literally 20 years later, and still cared about him, but there was no part of me that would ever in a million trillion years would rekindle the relationship—it was just, Guilt.

The week after I finished my yoga program he called, and we spoke on the phone for about an hour and a half as I listened to all of the mess that his life was and stayed compassionate and honest in my support for him (a lot of what I said was not what he wanted to hear). The entire conversation I was completely calm and clear, didn't feel any discomfort rising up in me, I didn't feel upset by the objectively painful news that he was sharing, I just was at peace and able to be supportive in whatever small, appropriate way I could. After the call, I just went right back to my life and didn't give the call or the details any additional thought. It was *remarkable* because at no time in the past 20 years would I have been able to be in that calm, clear state, and at no time prior would the call not have upset me for a considerable time afterwards. I'm certain that it was the work that I did in yoga, releasing and healing old wounds, that is the only reasonable explanation as to how I was able to not have the call affect me. It was unbelievable to me, because I had no awareness of when I let go of what I was holding on to, but obviously I did. It really works.

Depression

When we get stuck in these lower levels, this is Depression. By definition, we are stuck and we don't know how to get out. We are all doing our best from wherever we are, and sometimes our best can't figure out how to solve our problems. I think we have all been there, and I know that for me in those times, it was always seemingly the work of angels that got me through. I am not a PhD nor a Psychiatrist, and if you are struggling with Depression, please reach out for help. Just don't stop asking for help, please, and don't stop trying to get out of the darkness. Here are some things that I know from my own struggles:

1. Remember that you *can get better*. You are a miracle of life, the fact that you even exist as a human being is FREAKING MIRACULOUS. You ARE LIFE. And inherently in all life there is growth and possibilities.

2. Don't forget to ask for help, and don't stop asking for help. Angels (aka people who love you for no reason at all) are all around.

3. Learn about Anti-Fragilization and inform those around you about how you do not want to be fragilized.

4. Practice all 5 Pillars—especially self care, self compassion and kindness for others. It primes the pump!

5. Don't give up, just keep practicing all of these practices!

I've mentioned a few times one of the darkest times in my life, when I first got to college, deeply in love and deeply co-dependent, losing my love to drug addiction. The pain and desperation to help him was incapacitating and I was stuck very deep in Shame, Guilt, Apathy and Fear.

Fortunately I somehow ended up with the best friend and roommate I could've imagined, truly an angel, who held space for my pain and supported me through those dark times and literally kept me alive. I'd come home and walk in the door and without saying a word she would start to cry before I would start to cry. I remember one time after getting off the phone with Josh when he was high, I was in so much unbearable pain just staring at the window with the urge to just throw myself out of it because I simply needed the pain to stop, and she walked in and just wrapped me in her arms and held me and cried with me.

She got me through the worst, most tenuous moments, gave me her love, her spiritual strength, and it's absolutely what enabled me to get through those first years while I struggled with loving him and thinking that I needed him and that I needed to somehow save him, and yet, I couldn't. Sometimes, we need to remember to rely on our angels.

Chapter 8

ANGER

"Anger is precious. A silverback uses his anger to maintain order and warn his troop of danger. When my father beat his chest, it was to say, Beware, listen, I am in charge. I am angry to protect you, because that is what I was born to do.
Here in my domain, there is no one to protect."

–Katherine Applegate, The One and Only Ivan

Anger is human and we need to realize both its utility and its consequences. If we are angry, we are heated up, ready to fight. On the back side of Anger, we are scared or anxious, and we are pulling back, ready to run. Both anger and fear are responses to pain or fear of pain and impact our Spiritual Strength, as we are off balance, one way or the other, and inherently in a weakened position. It doesn't always feel that way thanks to our mind's perception of anger and the extra energy that comes with it, but trust me, we make horrible decisions when we are angry and we cause a lot of unnecessary damage.

When we are angry, we are in the midst of our Fight or Flight reflex. Our adrenalin is pumping, blood flow increases to our arms and legs, and we are in the primal part of our brain. Survival is the goal. Anger is *useful* when we need to physically protect ourselves or someone that we love. The problem is, our mind is saying *threat* in response to something that rarely is an actual physical threat. Our mind perceives threats all the time, and if we aren't skillful as we talked about on Courage, we can go down an unskillful, destructive path with our Anger.

Anger exists to cause damage—and if there isn't someone to physically fight off, that destructive energy is going to land on another target. Even if it is just words said in Anger, they will do damage. And if we just hold it inside of ourselves, it will do damage to us.

We need to embrace our Anger and allow it to rise up—feel the feeling and accept it for what it is—a sign that something isn't on track for us. Before we act out of Anger we need to mindfully check in and see if there is an actual physical threat—if there is not an actual physical threat we need to figure out how we can use the energy from our Anger in a constructive way. Asking ourselves, why is this threatening me so much and fully owning all of the answer—no blame.

If there is an actual physical threat, the Anger will be even more intense and fast and it will be harder to be mindful. I experienced this a few weeks ago when I was driving my kids to school. I was in the middle lane on the Cross County Highway going around a pretty sharp curve, but not so sharp that you drop under 60 mph. A car passed me on the left going considerably faster and then inexplicably cut right in front of me and slowed down. It was completely out of nowhere, not anything that any normal driver would do, and incredibly dangerous. I swerved out of the middle lane into the now open passing lane and passed the car in one second flat—it all happened so fast and it was scary. As I was passing the car I was ANGRY. In my head I was like, "Are you trying to kill my family?!?", completely enraged as I went by the driver. The second I saw the driver, an older woman with wide eyes who was apologetically waving a "I'm so terribly sorry, *mea culpa*," I instantly remembered to be mindful again and to diffuse the anger. I don't know what the heck was going on with that woman but she knew she had made a horrible mistake . . . and fortunately we all made it through and that moment was over. Anger was not useful anymore.

I immediately softened, turned my opened WTF hand into an "I Love You" sign and sailed past her . . . then turned on some dance music and shook off all of the adrenalin of the situation. I also used it as a teachable moment to the kids and diffused some of the energy explaining to them everything that had happened both externally on the road and internally in my head (and body!) as I navigated my fear and anger reaction.

Continuing to be Angry after a moment has passed serves no positive purpose. The sooner that you can allow it to come up, accept that yes, I am Angry, and then figure out how to forgive the person and let the love come back into your heart, the sooner you will be strong again.

Whenever I am Angry I know I have work to do. No matter the faults of others in my life, if I can not find Compassion regardless of their behavior, I know that is on me. No exceptions.

As I will continue to hammer home, Anger is a weakened spiritual state. I know, sometime it can feel *so good* to act out of Anger. There is a lot of energy that comes with it so it feels like power, and tearing down whoever is on the receiving end seems to our mind to be *exactly* what they deserve after *what they have done*. But our mind's perception of all of that, the blame, the shame, the power, is all *wrong*. As I am sure most of us have discovered, we make horrible choices when we are angry. We sabotage ourselves and others because we are acting out of our pain. The energy behind anything that we do out of Anger will be toxic. The perception of it feeling good is just an illusion, and we know it. It only feels good because on the inside we are hurting, and letting it out is the natural spilling over . . . but since we *know* that it is doing damage, know that too is all going to come back to us one way or another. We need to act out of Bravery and Love and Gratitude at all times to have that positive juju be what we are putting out there, because that is definitely what we want to get back.

Acting out of Anger always has destructive consequences—anyone who is around us when we act of our Anger will feel that energy, and it will not feel safe. If someone else is angry as well, it inflames the situation. If someone is vulnerable, the Anger will scare them. This is really important to remember as a parent and in relationships.

Ultimately, we want our children to feel safe and worthy of love, and acting out of Anger will not support that goal. Yes, we hold our children accountable and let them know if their behavior was out of line and that there are consequences . . . but whenever we get Angry with them and act out of that state, it subverts the foundation that we are trying to lay. It scares them and hopefully by now we realize that we don't want our children to be afraid of us. We want them to trust us so we can have synergy in helping them live their best lives.

No one is perfect, so whenever we do act out of Anger, it is an opportunity to teach them that we are all human, apologize for how you acted and use it as a teaching opportunity. It is the perfect time to talk to them about how hard it is sometimes to handle our big feelings, and to show them that you take full responsibility for your mistakes just like you ask them to.

Anger isn't bad, it isn't anything to feel ashamed or guilty about, it is something to commit to rising up through.

Chapter 9

DESIRE AND PRIDE

The Earth provides enough to satisfy every man's need, but not every man's greed.

–Mahatma Gandhi

Desire is another very human emotion. Let's call it a "Wanting". It clearly spurs our evolution, because if we didn't want for anything more, why would we bother to grow? So it seems like a positive, right?

Actually, Desire is a negative, weakened state, as opposed to a positive one. It stems from "wanting" because there is "not enough"—it is the opposite of Gratitude and born out of ignorance. There is always "enough", we are just looking at it from a flawed, limited perspective. This illusion of scarcity is one of the fundamental illnesses in our society. The way that our mind perceives that there can only be one winner and everyone else de facto is a loser if you didn't win.

I had this conversation recently with a friend and he pushed back big time. He said, "C'mon, give me a break. The Olympics are happening, and only one person can win the gold medal". And I said absolutely, only one person can take home the gold, but the mind's judgment that the only person who "won" was the gold winner was objectively ridiculous. Each person had a story and gained *something* from the experience, regardless if it were a victory or a lesson. We may not always get what we want, but we always get *something*. And to quote the Rolling Stones, I bet it is exactly what we *need*.

But let's just say for the sake of this conversation that you are sure that something could be better, so you are desiring it. We have to ask ourselves, when in a complete place of Gratitude, what is it that we are called to do? Can we start to see a bigger mission or purpose? If we are truly grateful for all that we have, and feel that grounded connection, it diffuses our desire and we can see clearly. Is what we are desiring in our highest good? Remembering that our highest good also takes into account how it impacts our entire world. Being of service is always a core component of our highest good. What do we envision for ourselves? What is in pursuit of our highest good? This is our vision.

Desire vs. Vision

We can envision goals and possible future outcomes and use this to inspire and guide us. This is a very different feeling than Desire. Desire is an attachment—it is us giving our power away to whatever it is that we are wanting. If we don't get it, we feel unfulfilled. If we get it, we feel fulfilled, but only temporarily. Desire is always an illusion that is a coverup for something that isn't whole in us and it is a weak, unhappy state. So, there is always something new that we will Desire.

There was a time not long ago that I had no awareness of the difference between Desire and Vision. Our mind alone can't really tell the difference. We need to be able to sense how we are feeling—are we feeling high or are we feeling low? How strong is the high feeling? If we imagine it taking a really long time to reach out goal, does that feel ok or does it feel bad? If there are any negative feelings associated with not getting what you want, that is Desire. And, it is working against your Spiritual Strength.

You can start to practice/ play with this a bit whenever you want to buy something. If you have a vision for what you are going to buy, you can see yourself using it and feel what it would be like to use it, that is cool. If you imagine yourself not getting it and it feels fine, that is cool. Maybe institute a policy of "wait a few hours or days or weeks before you buy something that you think you want" pay attention to how that feels.

Glamorization

Glamorization is when our mind assigns heightened value or worth onto something that we desire. We are convinced that this item, vacation, job, relationship will be the thing that makes everything perfect, it will be so good that we simply have to have it and it's worth whatever it is we have to go through to get it. Our mind convinces us that it is noble. But what happens when we get it? How fast does the luster wear off? If it wears off, that was glamorization.

Finding the Middle Path

Remember, there's this big, beautiful middle path where we have high standards for the goals that we set for ourselves while not attaching to them, allowing them to flow in how it all plays out, while we continue to put in our best effort. This is the dance of being present and blissful while having a grand vision for our life.

Both are equally important: the present bliss and the vision for the future. If we have a vision for the future but are not fulfilled in the present, we are unhappy and not doing our best work or living our best life. If we are blissful in the present moment but have no clear vision for the future, we can get stuck floundering our life away. It is *both* the present moment plus the vision that enables us to live our best life.

Our Desire can always teach us, in the same way that our Anger can teach us. Anything that we Desire is a clue as to where we have an opportunity to grow, and that is always a beautiful thing. Use it as a teachable, growing moment whenever you feel desire, and as you get better at knowing the difference between something that you Desire and something that sparks joy. Desire will always be needy, and the idea of not getting it will be upsetting, telling you that there is an attachment happening. Something that sparks joy will be easy and light and if it doesn't happen it will be fine (or the joy is in the process itself!) and you will be flexible. That is how to know you are on the right path.

Pride

Understanding Pride is important, because on the surface, much like Desire, it can seem positive. And indeed, it is much more positive than the lower states of Shame, Guilt, Fear etc. The problem with Pride is that it is fragile and shallow. It isn't based on deeper values, it is based on the Egoic assessment of comparison to others. It is therefore subject to insecurities, because the second something outside of yourself threatens the assessment of your worth, you feel the need to defend it or fight it. We literally perceive a threat to our security, in the same way we would perceive a physical threat. We covered this at length when we talked about Courage: we then get set into Fight or Flight which is never where we make our best decisions.

Our Ego feels Pride. We need to start to move out of our head and into our heart to feel the difference between Pride and self-love. Self-love feels like pride from the heart, instead of the head. From our heart we will connect with a deeper, intrinsic sense of worth that is independent of external factors—this is self-love or healthy self-esteem. From this place we can feel the difference between doing something because we are interested in a reward, as opposed to doing something because we feel unconditionally called to be of service, regardless of what comes of it. We need to be striving for this deep unconditional love, as opposed to shallow, conditional love, in all areas of our lives, in order to be able to find strength in the face of challenges. We are taking our power back as we figure out how to not allow anything outside of ourselves to "take away" from anything that we do. Feel self-love for your effort, your integrity, the intrinsic value of your service regardless of what accolades you get, but do not feel Pride in yourself compared to others. We are all equal, truly. None of this is personal, it isn't about you or me in the least.

When I was younger, I had a huge issue with Pride simply because I hadn't yet figured out who I really was and how to feel intrinsically worthy of love, or intrinsically "Good Enough". I always did really well in school, and typically got the highest grades on tests and assignments, but of course there were times when I didn't. And, understandably, when that happened, my peers would be excited. I know they didn't mean it (or, maybe some did, but it doesn't really matter), but when people got higher marks than I did, there would be a pretty big reaction around, "Wow, I did better than YOU DID?! HA! That's awesome! I did better than Pam!" Man, this felt so awful and uncomfortable as a kid. My heart knew to want to be happy for them, but my Pride was stung! Since I didn't really have a sense of what made me "enough", this was always a blow to my self worth. If my sense of worth came from the inside, as opposed to external validation, I wouldn't have been vulnerable the way that I was. Of course this is normal, but it is something that we can outgrown by learning how to differentiate between our intrinsic worth and the external comparison and validation our Ego seeks.

Chapter 10

RELATIONSHIPS

The fear of loss is the path to the dark side . . . attachment leads to jealousy, the shadow of greed that is...train yourself to let go of everything that you fear to lose.

—*Master Yoda*

Since no one is perfect, relationships are never going to be easy. You are going to bump into one another's sensitive spots, and you are going to bother and likely hurt each other. Most relationships are built on at least somewhat of a codependency, and depending on how healthy and aware the two people are, it can be quite functional or quite dysfunctional.

I'll share a bit about my relationship history because this is how I have learned all this—I've mostly been in long-term relationships—from 15-19 I was with my highschool sweetheart, Josh. From 19-22 I was with my college sweetheart. From 24-present I've been with my husband—we've been married 13 years. I have grown more from my relationships than from anything else in my life. The challenges that they presented, in figuring out who I was, what my values were, what my issues were, and how we could weather the stormy times were both the most painful and the most empowering opportunities in my life.

It was the summer before my junior year in high school, when I was 15, that I fell head over heels in love. I met Josh, a boy so charismatic, so smart, so handsome, and so in love with ME (?!?) that I was toast from the beginning. We were together over the next four years in total, through a lot of tough times. Shortly after we first started dating, my mom became very sick, and there were almost two years of fear and pain that fortunately my mother made it through...but during that time, Josh was my rock. He loved me and gave me strength to get through my mother's illness. He also was quickly spiraling into dysfunctional behavior (or behavior that existed before I met him was being revealed), that by any of my standards was unacceptable, but somehow it was balanced by lots of excitement and fun and love and support . . . so I compartmentalized the areas of concern and continued the relationship. I loved him with my whole heart, and as the years went on and I went to college, I've already shared that it became obvious that he was quite sick. I didn't have the skills on any level to untangle my concept of who I was and how safe I was or how worthy of love I was from that relationship . . . so I didn't know what to do about all of the pain and fear I was feeling. If I stayed, I was haunted by intense pain and fear, and if I left the relationship I was haunted by intense pain and fear.

It goes without saying that a dysfunctional, codependent relationship like this, where I had no real sense of self and was relying on the relationship for the validation of my worthiness of love and feeling safe, is extremely fragile and unhealthy. Any relationship where we are relying on someone else to make us happy and feel safe is destined to hit a wall. As Josh fell deeper into his illness, I fell deeper into my despair and the urgency grew to figure out a path out of the relationship. I will never forget all of my attempts that Sophomore year at Yale, different therapists, AL-ANON Meetings, trying everything possible to find a way to get out. Finally I met with a therapist who said to me, you need to develop a relationship with yourself. And I went back to my dorm and wrote and wrote and wrote to figure out *what the hell that meant*. Because as soon as she said it, even though I had no idea what it meant, I knew it was true and I needed to figure it out.

I share all of this because depending on where you are in your life and in your spiritual health, this could help you or someone you know . . . and it is integral to having a healthy relationship. We need to have a healthy sense of our self to have any hope of having a healthy relationship. We need to start to figure out what our issues are, what our fears are, what our shame is, what our anger is, what our desires are, and then continue to work on the 5 pillars of this book: Courage, Compassion, Gratitude, Surrender and Openness/Curiosity.

When you define yourself, consciously or subconsciously, by a relationship—your self-worth and identity are intrinsically tied to the relationship as opposed to you as an individual—and when the relationship needs to end, it is heartbreaking and terrifying at the same time.

Ultimately, the goal is to move our relationships out of transactional state, where it is about what we want to get from the person and what they want to get from us (this fundamentally starts as wanting to feel safe and worthy of love), to a synergist state, where both individuals are whole and not needing or desiring anything from each other to be happy and feel safe. That means that you are strong enough so that even the most painful of situations, having someone you love who is unwell and you are unable to help them, can be accepted. That is the highest level of Spiritual Strength, where absolutely nothing outside of you, regardless of the pain, has the power to bring you down. Truly a fabulous goal to continue to move towards, but in the meantime . . . we are human.

The day to day of relationships is never going to be perfect, no matter how strong we get spiritually. We are human and there are going to be issues that are imperfect and where one person gets triggered or hurt. Our partner will let us down and hurt us at times, and we need to figure out how to navigate that pain with grace.

Let's take a simple example, a common trigger for new parents: the baby gets sick. As new parents, we have no idea how to gauge the seriousness of any illness, and it is scary. It triggers this very deep fear of not being able to keep our baby safe AND our Desire to keep them from suffering. These are primal, instinctive fears and desires that are very strong and intense. They bubble up and are literally unbearable in many cases. Learning how to notice when these get triggered and how to handle that energy in a constructive way, to stay clear and centered, is key to making the best decisions for your family. If we allow ourselves to be unskillful in dealing with our fear and pain, we will mishandle the situation and make it worse instead of better.

For example, if a new parent gets triggered by the fear and stress of having the baby be sick, they are much more likely to be short with their partner, make rash, unreasonable assessments and demands, and to stress the baby out by putting their toxic energy out into the environment. Babies and children always do as well as their parents do in any situation, so parents staying calm and clear is key to helping your children feel safe. So, if a parent feels themselves getting stressed over the baby getting sick, it is an opportunity for the parent to practice releasing the underlying negative energy (explained in the chapter 7) BEFORE acting.

If you are on the receiving end of such behavior, it is likely that you would get hurt in some way, because your partner won't be gentle with you, won't be reasonable or patient and/or won't be understanding and considerate of your feelings and wishes . . . and this is how a fight happens. One partner gets triggered, and then triggers the other by behaving out of their fear/anger/stress.

This is just one example to illustrate what happens in so many different ways in relationships . . . one person gets triggered and then triggers the other person, and both people end up feeling awful and "blaming" the other. This is also what kills a relationship—the feeling of love you once shared gets replaced with resentment. It is very common for marriages to turn into a "we are roommates with a ton of shared responsibilities who don't seem to like each other all that much" arrangement.

Most married people have experience in this department and it can happen even in tiny ways. Tiny ways are when the other person is just imperfect somehow: they leave the towel on the floor, they don't thank you for getting something for them, they aren't as gentle in their communication, they aren't validating of your feelings . . . and these small imperfections get a lot of attention from our mind thanks to the Negativity Bias.

Negativity Bias Revisited

Remember how research has shown that our brain is literally hardwired to notice, focus on, and remember the negative[14]? We talked a bit about this earlier. Obviously historically and evolutionarily speaking, this is another fabulous survival feature . . . but in our relationships,

---

[14]Negative information weighs more heavily on the brain: The negativity bias in evaluative categorizations. Ito, Tiffany A.; Larsen, Jeff T.; Smith, N. Kyle; Cacioppo, John T. Journal of Personality and Social Psychology, Vol 75(4), Oct 1998, 887–900.

it is the anti-survival feature. Our mind stores away all of the negatives and remembers them with much more intensity than the positives, whether we are aware of it or not. Overtime, if we are unaware and not actively overriding it, these negative experiences build up . . . and it takes less and less for us to get triggered by our partners. We get annoyed, frustrated and start to lose faith in them. And that is just from the little things!!

And then of course, in most relationships, there will be bigger issues that come up. Feelings will really be hurt, communication will break down and trust will be broken. That pain left unhealed turns into deep anger and resentment . . . and it needs to be dealt with. We cannot continue pretending that it is acceptable to live in a relationship where there is underlying anger and resentment. We must proactively take responsibility for healing our relationship, regardless of the faults of our partner. For our own sake, we must be the bigger person if necessary, and own fixing things.

Let me say this as clearly as possible, because it is *that important*, and something that I wish I knew all those early, tough years of marriage: *if I am angry or resentful in the least, it is 100% on me, and I have major work to do— regardless the faults of my partner.*

If *anything* has the power to make me upset, angry, irritated, lonely, it is *only because some part of me is allowing it.* It takes Courage and Openness and Compassion to go into that unknown of who we are, the part that is wounded, the part that we may have no idea exists . . . but it is there, it is beautiful and messy, and that is where we will find our power and happiness. It is on the other side of pain, so this journey can only be taken with a warrior's spirit, but *you can do it*, and *it is worth it.*

First, we begin by being mindful and if your partner does anything that "makes you feel" lousy, ask yourself what is going on and OWN your feelings. No blaming them for how you feel. Never, never, never. That doesn't mean that you don't hold them accountable for whatever happened, but you need to own your feelings. The second you allow anyone to "make you feel" any way, you are giving your power away . . . and we need to keep our power! We need to OWN our life!

The thing is, anything that anyone else says or does only has the power to "make us feel bad" if we are allowing it. I'm going to keep asking you to embrace the idea that no one has the power to make you feel any way, unless you allow it. So, if something feels bad, say to yourself, *"why am I allowing this to bother me?"*

Sometimes that question alone will dissipate the heaviness of the situation. You may see that you are simply tired or hungry or whatever and it has nothing to do with the other person at all. Once I started this practice, I was pretty much appalled at how often this was the case. It was all me. Turns out that I was quite the sensitive flower.

Sometimes, the question will illuminate an opportunity in yourself, an insecurity, that you can pay attention to, figure out and commit to healing. Maybe something about how your partner treated you brought up feelings of being unsafe, or not enough, and you can see how this is your issue, not necessarily theirs. And, in case it isn't in the front of your mind, no one is responsible for your happiness and feeling safe except you, so if you are looking for that from your partner, you are going to hit a wall. For real.

And then sometimes, the question will shine a light on how your relationship could be stronger and more functional. Perhaps communication skills could be improved, or a deeper commitment to core values could be a focus . . . but that is always an opportunity and something to be excited about, seriously! We already knew that they weren't perfect, and that our relationship isn't perfect, so wooo hooo, an opportunity to take it up a notch and make it even better! That is AWESOME.

So, when your mind wants to make any of this a negative because your feelings got hurt, tell your mind to zip it and lean in to figure out what is really going on. Journalling is an excellent practice to start to try and untangle the feelings and wounds that you are dealing with. It really is an opportunity to make your relationship stronger, every time something goes wrong. No blame, no shame, just Courage, Curiosity and Compassion.

Forgiveness and Repairing Trust

Now, whenever there is a bigger issue and feelings really get hurt, two things are vital: forgiveness and repairing trust. Remember we talked about this in the chapter on

Compassion, and it is worth going deeper into when we are talking about our relationships.

Many people get confused about forgiveness versus the repairing of trust. If someone hurts you, and you forgive them, that doesn't mean that you don't hold them accountable for what they did, nor does it mean that you allow them close enough to do the same thing again. You can forgive someone without repairing trust. Repairing trust refers to a process where who ever hurt you demonstrates that they understand enough or are sorry enough to make you feel that you can trust them again. You hold them accountable for behavior that was unhealthy in such a way that you feel safe around them again.

This is vital for a healthy relationship, but there will be times when it cannot happen, and there must be more distance in the relationship than there was before the hurt. This a different process than forgiveness—forgiveness is deeper and universal regardless of whether trust can be re-established. Understanding this difference enables us to feel safe enough to forgive anything, freeing our spirit from the weight of the wound, while knowing that we can do what we need to do to maintain the integrity of our space safely going forward. Forgiveness does not mean that you allow the person close enough to hurt you again.

You can tell if you have forgiven someone if you can think of them with love in your heart. If your heart closes at all or you feel your spirits drop when you think of them, you know you haven't really forgiven them, you are still wounded, and you are still giving them your power.

Keep your intention on forgiveness so you can get your power back.

You can tell if you need to repair trust because while you may be able to keep your heart open and send them compassion, you do not feel safe or comfortable being close to them again. You need to listen to that inner feeling and keep distance or do what you need to do to have the trust repaired. Your inner feeling will always tell you what you need to do.

Unconditional Love vs. Conditional Love vs. Attachment

When we fall in love, we glimpse the purity and the power that is true, unconditional love. It's the most magical feeling we have ever experienced . . . and then, most of us pretty much immediately **fall in fear** of losing it. That magical, powerful, pure "high" was so good that nothing scares us more than having it go away. So, as soon as anything starts to be imperfect, or we start to *imagine* it being imperfect, we get triggered and Compassion and connection goes out the window. Or, we may actually torpedo it ourselves intentionally because it scares us so much. This all goes hand in hand with the Negativity Bias we just discussed, but it has the deeper foundation of fear of losing that pure love that we just discovered. So on top of the Negativity Bias, we have the attachment to the person and all of the heaviness that comes with it.

Attachment is based in fear, as opposed to love. If you are in a place of true love, it won't fear losing the magic. It won't judge when the person makes mistakes. It won't get its feelings hurt when something isn't as considerate as it could've been. It won't be controlling.

ATTACHMENT is the root of all of those negative feelings

True love is fearless. True love is generous. True love is forgiving. True love accepts whatever IS—no matter how imperfect. And true love is STRONG. Strong enough to say goodbye if being close is no longer supporting you to shine bright.

Attachment makes unconditional love impossible. That's because if we are attached, there will be expectations and needs/demands that we are placing on the other person. And, of course, with expectation or needs/demands, there will be disappointments and pain, which takes us out of Compassion.

In between attachment and unconditional love, we have conditional love. Conditional love is when we love the other person *only in certain conditions*. If they treat us a certain way, serve us a certain way, speak to us a certain way . . . but if something isn't "right", we fall out of love. This is very human, and I once had a brilliant, lovely Psychologist my husband and I were seeing (thank goodness for couples therapy!) say that there is no such thing as unconditional love as adults. Or maybe she meant that we can't expect it of ourselves or of the other person, in which case I would agree—we can't *expect* unconditional love. We can strive for it, though, and hold ourselves to that high standard. Even when our partner is really struggling and behaving in destructive ways, we can still strive to have unconditional love for them. That is compassion and the basis for true love.

She may also have meant that unconditional love is not romantic love, and romantic love cannot be unconditional. That I agree with completely. Romantic love is conditional—we will feel Romantic Love for someone on the conditions that we still are attracted to them. If we are no longer attracted to them, we cannot force romantic love. This is how you can still love someone unconditionally, but decide that you no longer feel that it is right to stay in a romantic relationship with them. That is a real and beautiful decision in my humble opinion. Love is love and attraction is attraction. It is what it is and not of this world.

Compassion without Enabling

It isn't your job to fix anyone. It is your job to always care about the wellbeing of others, aka be Compassionate. I will keep encouraging you to look for the big, beautiful middle path that provides us with the answers when we are stuck—in this case, it is where we can practice Compassion without enabling destructive behavior, and it is an art. It is an art because you have to feel it from the inside out, as opposed to being able to objectively have a map how to navigate the situation. No one can look at the situation and judge how you are handling it, you need to feel it out for yourself.

It is like fishing, if you have ever fished. There is an art to giving just enough of the line, and then taking just enough back, in order to reel in the fish. Too hard or too soft, you lose the fish. You have to feel the line, feel the pull and release of the fish, to know how to gracefully and effectively land the fish.

I am not making light of being in love with someone who is engaged in destructive behavior, or loving people who have committed suicide or have been lost to drugs or other seemingly senseless or avoidable tragedies. The grief involved in those situations is deep and of course our mind wants to avoid that pain at all costs, even if it means being out of alignment with our truths and engaging in enabling behavior if it means a chance at saving their life.

The reality is, other people's lives are out of our hands, regardless of how much we love them and how much we want to help them. And while our fear and pain may make us want to be extra supportive, which end up being enabling, doing anything out of fear or pain will always end up moving us in a negative direction. And we will be heading deeper into the guilt, fear and pain.

For many years, I carried around the guilt of an analogy that went something like this: I was in a boat in the middle of a lake with my best friend and he went overboard. He started to drown. At what point would a good person stop trying to save their best friend? At what point, even if you too are drowning, would it be acceptable to stop trying to save them? What if it were your child? Of course, my heart and head says NEVER! And so, when I "stopped trying" to save Josh all those years ago, and I had this analogy in my head and heart, the guilt that I felt was heavy and I didn't stop carrying it around until I had an epiphany: the boat analogy is completely wrong.

My new analogy synthesizes what I now know to be true—we are not responsible for saving anyone else from themselves. Enter, the rockwall. I love to rock climb and I realized one day that it is the perfect analogy to explain Compassionate Non-attachment and how to navigate someone we care about who is suffering and that we can't seem to help. Life is like climbing a rock wall, and we have to climb ourselves. When we love someone, we can cheer them on, send them tons of positive juju, even point out handholds and footholds and give some support from the bottom if they need it. But at the end of it all, each of us has to climb ourselves. If someone we love can't find the strength, clarity, power to climb, there is only so much we can do. And then, we need to do what we need to do to climb ourselves, and our own climb may take us away from them in time and space . . . but as long as we stay Compassionate with them in our hearts, we will always be connected and we will always be supporting them in the one way that we can. We need to Surrender obviously to what is out of our hands and Surrender to what is yet to come, and that is really, really hard.

Taking Things Personally

Then, there is taking things personally. Hopefully we all know that on some level, we are better off not taking things personally. We know that it doesn't serve us. Depending on our awareness and skill level, most of us are stuck on this somewhere, and it is in our best interest to keep taking this to a deeper and deeper level. It is easiest on the surface—if we run into someone that we don't know in the least, and they are nasty, it is the easiest to not personalize the interaction. They don't even know us, so how could their rude behavior really be about how awesome you are? But as we get to interactions that are more intimate, it gets harder and harder to not take things personally. (Wherever you are on this practice is exactly where you should be—you are where you are until you aren't there any more—zero judgments.)

When we are deeply connected to someone, we lose sight of how we are interacting. We lose sight of whether we are indeed taking things personally—when they act imperfectly, if we are deeply connected, we take it as a reflection of how they feel about us. It is hardest to not take things personally when we have a deep intimacy with someone—we lose perspective of the big picture as we operate from that place of closeness.

This can be little or it can be big—something as little as our partner being tired can trigger us if we take it personally. Why aren't they being warmer? Why aren't they being more enthusiastic about being with me? Well, if they are exhausted from a day of heavy lifting, it definitely doesn't have anything to do with you. But yet, often that exact situation would bum us out, "make us feel" less appreciated or desirable.

Whenever we allow someone else's behavior to "make us feel" anything we are taking it personally by definition! If we didn't take it personally, it wouldn't have any power over us! So what do we need to do to keep accepting and surrendering to the fact that no one is perfect, no one will perfectly handle situations, ourselves included, and when other people are imperfect it has nothing to do with us? Keep working on the 5 pillars and keep leveling up.

Loneliness and Rejection

The fear of rejection and loneliness is one of the most primal fears. We all want connection. Evolutionarily, in the days of old, if we were rejected we wouldn't survive, literally—we were reliant on our tribe for our basic needs. Rejection meant death. Rejection will always be painful, it is instinctively wired in, and the deeper the love you have for someone, the more painful their rejection will be. There is no way around that. Fearing that pain will keep us from living our life, so it's an opportunity to practice courage whenever this comes up.

Loneliness is not as intense as rejection, more of an underlying emptiness and lack of fulfillment, driven by our primal need to have connection. Because of our focus on our external world, we *think* that connection comes in the form of relationships. Our external world, however, is ultimately out of our control, and there will be times when we have to be alone. Learning to embrace being alone and overcoming your fear of loneliness is critical to tapping into your unlimited power and happiness.

One can experience the connection that we have to all life in a variety of ways, and ultimately this is the path to overcoming loneliness. Being in nature is healing because we intrinsically experience that connection. Traveling and experiencing other ways of life is another way that we feel that connection. Meditation and discovering who and what you really are is another. Once you discover the light and love within you, and connect with that, loneliness loses its power. Be particularly careful in today's world of social media and the internet as this creates a false sense of connection to others, and it blocks you from an authentic connection from the inside out.

Importance of Relationships

Even if we were to conquer our fears of rejection and loneliness, it is clear how much of our lives is about relationships. Whether it is in our personal lives or our professional lives, collaborating with others is how we are able to do things that we couldn't do on our own. Just like atoms bond to form molecules, people bond to form the invisible partnerships that exponentially increase potential. Learning how to have healthy relationships is one of the more fundamental things that humans need to learn how to do, aside from the MOST fundamental after survival, which is figuring out their inner peace.

First, we need to be stable as individuals, then we can have stable relationships. Fortunately, nothing in this world is perfect, it is all perfectly imperfect . . . and we can't let perfect be the enemy of the good. We can all commit to doing our best and always trying to do better. And, remember that everyone else is doing their best too.

In the book, The 5 Love Languages, Gary Chapman proposes five different main ways that people express and receive love, and that each of us has our own primary, preferred way—often different than our partner. For example, I am a quality time person, so for me, spending time together and sharing joy is how I express and want to receive love. My husband seems to be more of a words of affection kind of guy, so he naturally expresses love with kind words and that is how he looks to receive love. If we are speaking different languages, the two of us could both be trying to show each other love but the other person won't feel it. The other primary languages, Chapman says, are acts of service, gifts and physical touch—important to keep in mind and a book that definitely helped me learn how to connect better both with myself and with my husband.

It is also really important to revisit our discussion on Desire vs. Vision—we need to keep an eye on the Desires we are placing on a relationship and call ourselves out when they are coming from that weakened place. Our Desires will always weaken a relationship. Having a vision, however, and collaboratively working towards that vision, will strengthen a relationship. It's quite a powerful tool for evolving our relationships!

Relationship Skills

We talked a bit about DBT skills in our chapter on Courage and it's helpful to mention a few more here. One of the four main areas of DBT skills is interpersonal effectiveness and these three simple skills are incredibly powerful in practice:[15]

DEAR MAN - quick skill for getting your needs met

When something is off and we need to fix it, this is the go-to skill. It works as a parent, friend, partner, any relationship really. Practice these action items and get more skillful at each and your ability to navigate conflict with grace will markedly improve.

> D: Describe Situation
> E: Express how you feel about situation
> A: Assert Needs and Limits
> R: Reinforce/Reward
> M: be Mindful/ Focused
> A: Act confident
> N: Negotiate

Suppose, hypothetically speaking, that I booked 6am flight for our family vacation, and my husband Roger thought that was insane and really felt like he couldn't

---

[15]Marsha M. Linehan, DBT Skills Training Manual (Guilford Publications, Inc.: 2014).

handle traveling that early. He could use DEARMAN to try and get me to change the flight. He could describe the situation and how he feels about the situation, asserting that he needs 8 hours sleep and that he his limit for a morning flight is 9am, 8am at the earliest. He could be really clear on how I would be rewarded for working with him on this—he would really appreciate it, be happy with me, I'd get a hug and a kiss and he could assure me that he would be an excellent, easy traveler if we pushed the flight back. By staying mindful and focused, he would avoid bringing up unrelated things that I do that he finds unhelpful or annoying (I am sure that there are plenty!). He could act confident, like he really believes this is the best way to go. And then, he could negotiate to get to a more desirable flight time. I am certain that if he followed these steps, he would be successful in getting me to change to a slightly later flight, if there were reasonably priced options available. DEARMAN is a very skillful way to handle a conflict and it really is effective.

GIVE - quick skill for strong relationships

We all want to have strong relationships and these simple skills lay a strong foundation. I teach them to my children and love watching how well they works.

G: Gentle
I: Interested
V: Validating
E: Easy Manner

In the moment, to treat each other gently, to be interested in each other and make sure the other person feels heard, to validate each other's feelings and be easy with each other as things ebb and flow with both victories and challenges is like a magic recipe for a healthy relationship. When I first learned this, I realized that I often was a horrible invalidator. I'd roll my eyes, sigh, be very judgmental about feelings, when I needed to be practicing validation. It was hard and awkward at first, but I have been practicing and fortunately, practice makes progress! I am getting much better and it makes a big difference in the dynamic of relationships because the other person feels seen and heard.

FAST - quick skill for maintaining self respect

F: Fair
A: No Apologies
S: Stick to Values
T: Truthful

If we practice being fair, not apologizing for our truth, sticking to our deeper values and being honest, we will be able to maintain the integrity of our self respect. Self respect and self compassion go hand in hand and are integral to building our Spiritual Strength.

Regardless of which practices you choose, keep practicing them . . . and keep remembering that you are connected to all life. This is a powerful knowing.

Nurturing a long term relationship takes a lot of work, a lot of wisdom and a lot of patience and forgiveness . . . and obviously the more Spiritual Strength each of you have, the more powerful and happy the relationship will be. It is always worth the effort when both people are committed to the relationship. If one person is not committed to working on the relationship, then that is an insurmountable problem. That is one of the reasons wise coaches say to focus on the commitment as opposed to whatever any given conflict is - by focusing on the commitment you have a foundation for growth.

The main two fundamental promises my husband and I make to each other are to always make sure the other person feels heard and to always care about the other person's feelings, even if they make no sense. By focusing on validation and empathy, we will have a connection that keeps us grounded through whatever is the conflict at hand. And of course, there is no avoiding conflict in a relationship!

Chapter 11

EVOLUTION

The closest we ever get to perfection is in the process of our evolution.

— *Pamela Palladino Gold*

I remember being three or four and lying in bed, and I remember the exact short ruffled pajamas I was wearing and the fan in my window in my old house on Mayer Drive and it was so hot and uncomfortable ... and I remember wiggling my tongue, and I remember exactly how it felt and tracing it back and wondering *how the heck can I do that?* and *who am I* and *why am I here in this body?* (I went deep early)

I seemed to have this innate eternal quest to figure out the meaning of life ... but never would I've thought that my discovery would end up being oh. so. simple. Knowing everything that I know now, the meaning of life is simply to *live*. And to *live* means to show up *in each moment* with infinite love in your heart and infinite enthusiasm and inspiration to do whatever work is at hand. To be of service to the larger good. It is this effort, borne out of love and truth, that is the force of life that creates the process of evolution.

If you look around and *really look*, I bet you can see this force at work, on both the micro and macro level. In the microcosm, on the cellular level, in our ecosystem, with random acts of kindness—this is evolution happening all around us. We are part of it.

Evolution in general isn't linear. It isn't always moving towards what we judge as higher levels of order and complexity when we are are watching it as closely as possible. There are always patterns that we can't see, until we "level up" with our awareness. It is only when we can look at it from afar, seeing the big picture, that the patterns emerge and we have a shot of making sense of it all.

Our own evolution is equally non-linear. We all have experienced how often times our greatest strengths emerged from our greatest failures. It seemed on the surface that we were being beat down, but it was all part of the process of rising up. It is only from challenges that we evolve.

Participating in evolution means that we are contributing to this process both within ourselves and outside of ourselves. As our awareness expands beyond only seeing our own needs, we understand higher truths and we are able to contribute on a higher and higher level. So first, we must commit to expanding our awareness, doing these Spiritual Strength practices, yes to get stronger and stronger, to stay clear and powerful and inspired, and also at the same time to support our epiphanies and expanded awareness. And then, as our awareness expands, we will have more and more clarity on how we can support evolution outside of ourselves in the big, beautiful world. Transitioning from it being all about us, to realizing that life isn't remotely personal . . . and there are infinite opportunities to be of service in supporting what we are all a part of, LIFE.

There are infinite opportunities as we go about our day to be of service to others, that take no time at all. Sometimes it is something as small as a smile, holding a door, paying someone a compliment. Maybe it is something bigger, creating a new solution to a major problem facing humanity or being a leader in social justice. There is no single path or an act too small— indeed, an entire lifetime of small moments amounts to a huge amount of evolution that perhaps you never get to see. The key is both maintaining our individual integrity while surrendering to whatever life asks of you with no expectation of anything in return . . . being of service and contributing to the greater good while having no attachment to the result of the work, and no egoic pride associated with how others view you for your "good deeds." This is what is what allows the flow of life and evolution to be at its maximum power.

It is clear that we can't hope to evolve to the maximum of our potential without great Spiritual Strength. It isn't easy to resist being weighed down by the pain and the challenges of life, and instead to rise up to a more powerful state with each challenge faced . . . being able to affect great change in the face of great adversity. This is the Power that we all need to aspire to. It is the Power of inner peace, and it will lead to our greatest evolution.

Truly, unlocking unlimited power and happiness.

47763835R00109

Made in the USA
San Bernardino, CA
07 April 2017